Cybersecurity Careers

Kathryn Hulick

ReferencePoint
Press®

San Diego, CA

About the Author

Kathryn Hulick began her career with an adventure. She served two years in the Peace Corps in Kyrgyzstan, teaching English. When she returned to the United States, she began writing books and articles for kids. Technology and science are her favorite topics. Look for her books: *Careers in Robotics*, *Robotics Engineer*, and *Virtual Reality Developer*. She also contributes regularly to *Muse* magazine and the Science News for Students website. She enjoys hiking, painting, reading, and working in her garden. She lives in Massachusetts with her husband, son, and dog.

For more information, contact:
ReferencePoint Press, Inc.
PO Box 27779
San Diego, CA 92198
www.ReferencePointPress.com

Picture Credits:

Cover: PeopleImages/iStockphoto.com
 6: Maury Aaseng
19: REDPIXEL.PL/Shutterstock.com
37: ProStockStudio/Shutterstock.com
46: Mike Fouque/Shutterstock.com
61: Jacob Lund/Shutterstock.com

LIBRARY OF CONGRESS CATALOGING-IN-PUBLICATION DATA

Names: Hulick, Kathryn, author.
Title: Cybersecurity Careers/by Kathryn Hulick.
Description: San Diego, CA: ReferencePoint Press, Inc., [2019] | Series: STEM Careers | Includes bibliographical references and index. | Audience: Grades 9 to 12.
Identifiers: LCCN 2018022047 (print) | LCCN 2018022286 (ebook) | ISBN 9781682824306 (eBook) | ISBN 9781682824290 (hardback)
Subjects: LCSH: Computer networks—Security measures—Vocational guidance—Juvenile literature. | Data protection—Vocational guidance—Juvenile literature. | Computer crimes—Prevention—Vocational guidance—Juvenile literature.
Classification: LCC TK5105.59 (ebook) | LCC TK5105.59 .H85 2019 (print) | DDC 005.8023—dc23
LC record available at https://lccn.loc.gov/2018022047

Contents

Introduction: The Dangers
of the Digital World   4

Information Security Analyst   8

Information Security Architect   16

Ethical Hacker   25

Cyber Incident Responder   33

Digital Forensics Investigator   42

Data Privacy Attorney   50

Security Auditor   58

Cryptologist   67

Interview with an Information
Security Architect   74

Other Jobs in Cybersecurity   77

Index   78

The Dangers of the Digital World

Digital devices such as cell phones, laptops, smart watches, fitness trackers, and more connect the world and make life more convenient. Many people have become so dependent on digital technology that they could not conduct their business or manage their daily lives without it. They sleep with smartphones by their pillows, as if the device were an extension of the body.

The more people rely on technology, however, the more vulnerable they become to data breaches or technology failures. "In the digital economy, virtually everything is connected. That means that everything is at risk for a cyberattack," said former chair of the Federal Communications Commission Tom Wheeler during a 2018 Brookings Institution panel discussion. Cybersecurity is a field devoted to making sure that people's digital possessions and transactions remain safe and secure.

Cyberattackers and Defenders

High-profile hacks have become common in recent years. In 2016 Yahoo! revealed that hackers had stolen user information—including names, e-mail addresses, phone numbers, and more—from over 1 billion Yahoo! accounts. Cyberattackers also spread viruses and malware that interfere with people's devices. They hold company databases or personal files for ransom. They take over people's digital identities in order to steal money. They pose as friends, family, banks, or the government in order to entice people into fraudulent schemes. These criminals, also called "black hats," may be lone individuals or may represent extensive networks of organized crime—or the efforts of foreign governments. Fears of cyberterrorism and cybercrime are more pervasive among Americans today than fears of biological warfare or being murdered, according to a 2015 study by researchers at Chapman University in California. And in 2016, 32 percent of organizations reported cybercrime losses, making this the second-most-reported financial crime, according to a report from PricewaterhouseCoopers.

Cybersecurity, like real-world security, relies on a series of safeguards intended to protect sensitive items and trigger a response if any breach or other suspicious event occurs. However, cyberspace is much more difficult to protect than real space. In the real world, a thief must travel to the location where the goods are kept. In the digital world, all a thief needs is access to the Internet. Attackers can attempt to break in from almost anywhere in the world. Plus, a cyberattacker can easily disguise his or her identity and location, making it nearly impossible to trace where the attack came from. In the real world, a thief can only take what he or she can carry. And a physical item cannot easily be duplicated. A cyberattacker can quickly copy or transfer huge amounts of data. Often, the breach is not immediately obvious.

Protecting items from attack is only half of the security problem. Locking something away so safely that no one can get to it would protect that item but would not be very practical. Security systems must allow access to the right person or people. Making access easy for real users but difficult for imposters is a very tough problem. In the digital world, companies striving for convenience for their customers may end up sacrificing security.

Complicating matters, the rules about cybersecurity are still being written. The Internet has only existed for a few decades, and new digital technologies are being developed at a dizzying pace. Security for these technologies often lags behind adoption. New applications (apps) or devices may not store or use personal information appropriately. But if the technology is helpful or fun enough, most people will use it anyway. Governments, regulators, and industry groups are slow to introduce laws and regulations that will help protect people and their data in the fast-paced, ever-changing digital world.

Top Cities for Cybersecurity Salaries

		Average salary
1.	Minneapolis, MN	$127,757
2.	Seattle, WA	$119,349
3.	San Francisco, CA	$119,346
4.	Dallas, TX	$117,890
5.	Denver, CO	$117,308
6.	Chicago, IL	$111,303
7.	Austin, TX	$110,190
8.	Salt Lake City, UT	$106,207
9.	New York, NY	$102,271
10.	San Jose, CA	$99,075
11.	San Diego, CA	$98,303
12.	Washington, DC	$92,191
13.	Boston, MA	$88,453
14.	Los Angeles, CA	$86,072
15.	Arlington, VA	$74,254

Source: University of San Diego, "Cyber Security Stats That Prove We Need More Experts with Computerr Security Degrees," 2018. https://onlinedegrees.sandiego.edu.

Welcome to the Wild West

In some ways, the digital world is like the Wild West, which was a new, exciting, largely lawless place. There were not enough sheriffs and deputies to keep all the bandits at bay. In cybersecurity today, there are not enough professionals with the right skills to stop all the cybercriminals. Nearly every industry in the world, from banking to education to health care, now relies on digital technology in one form or another and needs to make sure this technology is secure. But skilled cybersecurity experts are hard to find. "Unfortunately, the pipeline of security talent isn't where it needs to be to help curb the cybercrime epidemic," said Robert Herjavec in a 2017 jobs report by industry analyst Cybersecurity Ventures. "Until we can rectify the quality of education and training that our new cyber experts receive, we will continue to be outpaced by the Black Hats."

In 2017 the unemployment rate in the cybersecurity field dropped to 0 percent, according to Cybersecurity Ventures. The same report also predicted 3.5 million unfilled cybersecurity jobs by 2021. In another report on employment by the same firm, chief executive officer Frank Zinghini of Applied Visions says, "Opportunities for jobs in the cybersecurity sector are abundant, and far outstrip the available talent to fill them." As a result, cybersecurity professionals have excellent prospects for finding a job and often earn very high salaries.

Cybersecurity jobs involve protecting sensitive, valuable, or important information and fighting cybercrime. Following this career path means taking on great responsibility. A mistake in cybersecurity could cost a company or individuals huge amounts of money or forever tarnish someone's reputation. For the right person, though, a career in cybersecurity offers a sense of fulfillment and plenty of excitement. By outsmarting and stopping the "bad guys," a successful cybersecurity professional makes the world a safer and better place.

Information Security Analyst

What Does an Information Security Analyst Do?

Information security analysts are the security guards of the digital world. Depending on the organization, a person in this role may be called an information security coordinator, consultant, facilitator, liaison, officer, or manager. While a regular security guard patrols a building or outdoor area, an information security analyst monitors digital files, devices, databases, or networks, watching for suspicious activity. The goal is to keep sensitive digital information from falling into the wrong hands.

Information security analysts make life difficult for would-be data thieves and spies. "Basically, we play cops and robbers all day," Tony Sanchez, an information security analyst at the Johns Hopkins University Applied Physics Laboratory, told the author. Information security "cops" go after "robbers" that may attempt to break into a secured digital environment.

Cyberattacks are silent. Human senses such as sight and hearing cannot detect them. Often, a compa-

8

ny will not even realize an attack has occurred until several months afterward, when the damage has already been done. Information security analysts rely on a variety of software solutions and digital tools that help watch for attacks and send alerts when suspicious activity occurs. For example, antivirus software regularly scans computer systems for malicious code or dangerous files.

Information security analysts also utilize tools that secure data or authenticate users. Data encryption programs scramble sensitive information. Only someone with the right credentials can unscramble the data to look at it or use it. A firewall is a tool that separates one network from another in order to secure data. A company may use a firewall to protect an internal network of employees' computers from the public Internet. The firewall allows employees to use the Internet but keeps Internet users from being able to access data on the private network. Active Directory is a Windows tool that identifies and authorizes users on a network. It gives permission to perform certain tasks. For example, this tool may only allow people with administrator credentials to install new software on computers on the network. An information security analyst must understand how to install and maintain all of these tools and must stay up-to-date as new tools are developed.

On a typical day, an information security analyst looks at all the tools his or her company is using for security monitoring. Any alerts that come in must be investigated and resolved. Richard Cassidy is a security architect at Alert Logic, a security services company. In a company video, he describes what security analysts on his team do each day: "An analyst when they start their shift will always receive a handover from the night shift to ensure they are well aware of any major incidents or even normal incidents raised during the night." Any unresolved cases must be addressed. If a cyberattack does occur, an information security analyst must try to reduce the damage. Afterward, the analyst may be responsible for investigating what happened and preparing reports for management.

Many information security analysts help develop and write security standards for their company or organization and make recommendations for any new security measures that should be implemented. They often help educate colleagues on proper security precautions and may provide help desk assistance to users who encounter security problems.

How Do You Become an Information Security Analyst?

Education

At most companies, information security analysts work in a very specialized role within the broader information technology (IT) department. A student looking to work in this specialized position should first focus on building strong IT skills. At the high school level, students should take classes in computer programming, computer science, and network technology if they are available. General math and science classes are helpful as well.

At the college level, a bachelor's degree in computer science, IT, or another computer-related field is the best way to prepare. A two-year associate's degree in IT—for example, in computer network administration—can also help kick off a successful career, though it will take longer to gain the experience and skills necessary to work as an information security analyst. Finally, if a student is really serious about information security, he or she may want to consider master's degree programs that focus on this area.

When choosing an information security course or degree program, professors who also have real-world experience working in the field will provide the best guidance. "You want a program that not only focuses on theory but also gives you hands-on experience," Christopher M. Flatley of the security consulting company Lead Cyber Solutions says in a company video. He adds, "Make sure [the program] has a lab or some simulated environment where you'll actually get real world experience on servers, network switches, and routing protocols."

Once a person graduates and starts working as an information security analyst, he or she will need to continue to learn and train on new tools and technologies as they become available. The company where a person works may offer training programs. Training in specific security tools is also available online, often for free.

Certification and Licensing

Some information security analysts get by without certifications. Increasingly, though, companies require certifications when hiring new analysts. Having one or two certifications in IT or information security will certainly set an applicant apart from others who do not have these credentials. "Certifications show a continuing education and a commitment to knowing the subject . . . a company can hire you without having any worry that the theory you learned in the classroom might not translate to the real world," says Flatley in the same video. Maintaining most certifications means completing as many as forty hours of training every year. Common, well-respected certifications for information security analysts include Certified Information Systems Security Professional (CISSP), Certified in Risk and Information Systems Control (CRISC), GIAC Security Essentials (GSEC), and CompTIA Security+.

Networking and Internships

The more hands-on experience and training a person can gain in information security, the better off he or she will be when looking for a job. Internships are one of the best ways to gain work experience and often lead to a permanent job offer with the company. Companies in a wide variety of industries are looking to hire information security interns.

Internships also offer an opportunity to network with others already working in the information security field. Joining a professional organization focused on information security or attending a conference for professionals in the field is another great way to network. In a virtual meet-up sponsored by the Information Systems Security Association (ISSA), David Dumas, senior principal in security risk management at Verizon, says, "If you want to get into this field, one of the best things to do is to go hang around with people who are in the field."

Skills and Personality

Information security analysts typically do not know what types of problems they will face on any given day. This is a very reactive, problem-solving role that depends on quick thinking, strong analytical skills, and attention to detail. "If you like solving problems, you like sinking your teeth into something, digging into it, and figuring out what's going on, how it happened, and if it's something bad, how do we prevent it happening again, security is right up your alley," says Jason Schlemmer in the ISSA virtual meet-up. He is an information security analyst at Johns Hopkins University Applied Physics Laboratory. An information security analyst also needs to have a strong technical understanding of topics such as computer systems and network communications. Writing and speaking skills are important as well, since analysts often work on security documentation and training.

On the Job

Employers

Many information security analysts work in full-time positions for private companies or public organizations. All industries need information security professionals, but demand is greatest in the government as well as in the health care, financial, and communications industries. Many companies, especially small to medium-sized ones, do not hire their own information security staff. Instead, they work with security consulting firms, also called managed security providers. These businesses take care of the cybersecurity needs of a number of clients. Most information security analysts work at this type of company.

Working Conditions

Information security analysts almost always work within a larger IT department. Like other IT work, this is an office job that mainly involves sitting indoors at a computer. Most people in this role work full time and often put in extra time beyond the standard forty-hour workweek. Information security analysts may have to work shifts that fall outside of normal business hours or may have to handle emergencies that occur on nights or weekends. Analysts in consulting roles may be able to work from home.

Many more men than women work in cybersecurity. Minorities are underrepresented as well. Worldwide, women make up just 11 percent of the cybersecurity workforce, and minorities less than 12 percent. Meanwhile, companies struggle to fill open security positions. These facts have led many security professionals to look for ways to attract more women and minorities to the field. "Having a more diverse workforce creates a more diverse culture within the company. That's good for business," says Steven Ostrowski, a spokesperson for the trade association CompTIA, in an article on the Society for Human Resource Management website.

Earnings

Information security analysts earn excellent salaries. As of May 2016, the median wage for information security analysts in the United States was $92,600. On the low end, an analyst may earn around $53,760. But with additional education and work experience, the salary may reach almost $150,000. "In some places with high demand, the salary [for an information security analyst] can rocket up over $100,000 with four years of experience out of college," Dumas told the author. "I work out of my house and I make a decent living."

Opportunities for Advancement

Most people who become information security analysts already have three to five years of experience working in IT. The person may start out at the help desk or as a network or computer systems administrator. While in an entry-level position in IT, a person who shows the appropriate interest and aptitude may begin to specialize in security. An information security analyst also has plenty of potential for career growth. An analyst who enjoys the technical side of the job may become an information security architect or engineer who designs and implements new information security systems. An analyst who becomes an expert in the security needs of a particular industry may eventually work his or her way into upper management. The highest possible role is chief information security officer.

What Is the Future Outlook for Information Security Analysts?

Cyberattacks are becoming more and more frequent. The more these attacks occur, the more demand there will be for information security analysts who know how to stay one step ahead. The Bureau of Labor Statistics predicts 28 percent growth in this job through 2026. That is twice as much growth as all computer-related occupations and four times as much growth as predicted for all occupations. In a 2018 ranking of the ten best technology jobs, *U.S. News & World Report* placed information security analyst at number two. "There's always going to be room for another security analyst, always," predicts Sanchez in the ISSA virtual meet-up.

In many computer-related jobs, automated programs are taking over work that was once performed by humans. But in security, smart programs alone are not sufficient to get the job done. Security professionals must be able to think like human hackers and outsmart them. Dumas told the author, "You can't use computers and robots to do this. You need people with minds thinking outside the box."

Find Out More

CompTIA
3500 Lacey Rd., Suite 100
Downers Grove, IL 60515
website: www.comptia.org

This organization supports all IT professionals. The group sets industry standards, fosters skills development, and generates knowledge and insight for those working in the field.

Information Systems Security Association (ISSA)
1964 Gallows Rd., Suite 310
Vienna, VA 22182
website: www.issa.org

The ISSA is an international community devoted to helping cybersecurity professionals advance in their careers. The group organizes conferences, meet-ups, and other events for security professionals.

International Information System Security
Certification Consortium (ISC)^2
311 Park Place Blvd., Suite 400
Clearwater, FL 33759
website: www.isc2.org

This professional organization helps information security professionals learn, grow, and thrive. (ISC)^2 provides the well-respected CISSP certification as well as other forms of education and training.

SANS Institute
11200 Rockville Pike, Suite 200
North Bethesda, MD 20852
website: www.sans.org

This organization facilitates the sharing of important information and research among information security professionals. It also operates the Internet Storm Center, a free service that monitors the public Internet for malicious attacks.

Women's Society of Cyberjutsu
1405 S. Fern St., Suite 514
Arlington, VA 22202
website: http://womenscyberjutsu.org

This organization is devoted to empowering women to succeed in the cybersecurity field. It promises to train the next generation and help solve the gender divide in the field.

Information Security Architect

Information Security Architect

Minimum Educational Requirements
Master's degree preferred

Work Experience Required
At least five years

Personal Qualities
Problem-solving skills, leadership, communication, adaptability

Certification and Licensing
CISM, GSLC, and more

Working Conditions
Indoors at a computer

Salary Range
Around $84,122 to $154,987

Number of Jobs
Around 4,500 online job postings per year as of 2017

Future Job Outlook
Growth of 28 percent through 2026, much faster than most jobs*

* Numbers come from the Bureau of Labor Statistics listing for information security analysts, whose role is closely related to that of information security architects.

What Does an Information Security Architect Do?

Information security architects research, design, and maintain security systems. They oversee the implementation and testing of new security systems and play an important role in writing and enforcing security policies. This is a senior-level position with job responsibilities similar to those of an information security engineer or lead security engineer.

An information security architect is the person responsible for building or acquiring the software and tools that analysts use to keep an eye out for attacks. The architect must also figure out how to integrate those tools into the existing infrastructure. This task requires seeing the big picture of how all of an organization's security tools work together to respond to threats and predicting how the security system will interact with technology that has not been invented yet.

Information security architects typically oversee a team of analysts and engineers. They must manage their team's work and make decisions about who to hire or let go. The architect also manages security auditors or ethical hackers to test a security system. If tests find significant gaps or holes that could allow attack, the architect must determine how to close them.

The decisions an information security architect makes affect the entire company or organization. As a result, a person in this role must work closely with engineers, information technology (IT) architects, upper management, and even legal experts to help inform their decisions. Some of the most important decisions they make involve choosing which security technology to invest in. Once the company decides to use a new technology, the information security architect is responsible for working with the vendor to integrate it into existing systems.

New security technology does not always come from external vendors. Many security architects and engineers design or customize software solutions to fit their specific needs. They may need to design or write custom code to help keep watch over part of a system or to test for vulnerabilities. Fatima Rivera is an information security engineer at Google. In a company video, she describes a typical day on the job: "I spend quite a bit of time doing research about new security methodology. I spend some time coding, and I spend quite a bit of time doing analysis, looking at our team's detections."

How Do You Become an Information Security Architect?

Education

Preparing for the role of information security architect typically requires about ten years of education and work experience. The best

17

way to start out is with a bachelor's degree in computer science, IT, or engineering. These majors help provide a solid foundation in math, science, and technology. Programming is a very helpful skill to learn but is not essential. Many information security architect positions also require a master's degree in information security or computer science. Many people earn a bachelor's degree then work for several years in entry-level IT, engineering, or software developer positions before getting an advanced degree. "I would probably not recommend pursuing a [bachelor's] degree in security itself," says Jelena Magarasevic in a video by the security software development company Level 3 Communications, where she is director of security architecture. She explains that getting an engineering or networking degree first, then adding security training, gives students more options for their careers.

Certification and Licensing

Many employers look for certifications when hiring security professionals at all levels. By the time a professional has the work experience necessary to qualify for an information security architect role, he or she likely already has a few IT or security certifications in hand. However, more senior-level certifications are also available. For example, Certified Secure Software Lifecycle Professional (CSSLP) and Certified Information Security Manager (CISM) each identify someone who understands how to develop and oversee security systems, and GIAC Security Leadership (GSLC) recognizes management ability.

Volunteer Work, Internships, and Mentors

Getting hands-on experience with computers and networks is essential for someone who wants to eventually design methods to protect those computers and networks. Volunteer work and internships provide valuable experience. Any IT-related work will help, even if it is not focused on security. "If you can say you worked as an intern somewhere, or did computer work volunteering for your local church or boy scout troop or the YMCA, anything that makes you learn more about computers, then it shows

In addition to building or acquiring software and tools that analysts will use to spot attacks, information security architects also have to develop ways to integrate these tools into existing infrastructure.

you have initiative," David Hayes, an information security architect at Verizon, told the author.

Finding a mentor is another important step, especially for someone who hopes to work toward a senior-level position in the field. A mentor can help guide a security professional throughout his or her career. In an interview by the Bureau of Labor Statistics, Candy Alexander, a freelance cybersecurity consultant, suggests these approaches to finding one: "Go to meet-ups, or join user groups or professional associations to meet others in the cyber-security field. Latch on to those who are able to help and answer questions. Start talking to people and get your name out there; let them know that you're looking to get started. It's amazing how many people are willing to help if only you ask."

Skills and Personality

To succeed as an information security architect, a professional must acquire deep expertise in security, combined with broad general knowledge of IT. Some technical concepts that an information security architect must understand thoroughly include protocols, or the rules for how devices on a network communicate; encryption, or the use of codes to disguise data; and authentication and authorization, or the process of determining whether a user has permission to access something.

However, even the strongest set of technical skills will not help a security professional when it comes to leading a team or persuading others to accept his or her ideas. Soft skills in leadership, communication, and management are extremely important. Information security architects must also feel comfortable with unpredictability. Magarasevic says, "[Security] is a field that constantly changes. The threats are evolving. The bad actors in the security landscape are always coming up with new tools and new attack vectors." In the face of new threats, an information security architect must have the motivation and drive to learn new technologies and develop innovative solutions.

On the Job

Employers

Information security architects typically work as part of the management team at private companies or organizations. The industries that hire the most cybersecurity professionals include banking and finance, communications, and health care. Companies that provide security consulting services or develop security software also hire architects to manage the security of their own systems as well as those of their clients.

The US government is an important employer, offering a huge range of positions in information security in both military and nonmilitary roles. As a result, many information security architect jobs are located in or around Washington, DC. New York and San Francisco are two other important hubs.

Working Conditions

An information security architect is in a high-stakes position with a lot of responsibility. The work can be stressful and demanding. Most information security architects work forty hours or more per week, almost all indoors at a computer. They may have to put in time during nights or weekends to respond to a breach or other security incident. On the other hand, architects who have worked at the same company long enough may have earned the flexibility to work from home or make their own hours. The unpredictability of the job can also be very exciting. On a given day, a person in this role may need to handle a deeply technical problem, a procedural problem, or a business problem.

The issue of underrepresentation of women and minorities in cybersecurity is dire when it comes to senior-level positions. In an article on the Society for Human Resource Management website, Deborah Hurley, who teaches cybersecurity courses at Brown University, describes what happens to the women who do end up beginning careers in technology, "Some women drop out. Others hang in there but do not receive the same recognition, training or opportunities as their male colleagues." The industry is working hard to address the shortage of women and minorities in technical leadership positions. One way to address the problem is to pair new hires with strong role models and mentors within the organization. Many people in the field are optimistic that change is on the way.

Earnings

Information security architects earn excellent salaries and benefits. In general, the compensation for a job in security is higher than the compensation for a similar level of job in another area of IT. Expertise in web security and encryption tends to lead to the highest salaries. PayScale, a provider of salary and compensation information, estimates that professionals in this role earn about $84,122 to $154,987. Since this is a senior-level role, many also earn substantial yearly bonuses or participate in profit sharing, which can add as much as another $25,000 to annual earnings.

Career Path

The typical path to becoming an information security architect begins in either software development or IT. Someone with a computer science education will typically start out as a developer or software engineer and will advance from there to a position as an information security engineer. A professional with a degree in IT will typically start with an entry-level position at the help desk or as a network or system administrator before moving up to become an information security analyst or engineer. Typically, a person will need at least five years of experience, and perhaps more, in these entry-level and mid-career positions before earning a promotion to information security architect. From there, the path continues into upper management. "I think the ultimate step for a security professional is becoming a Chief Security Officer and having the ultimate accountability for all the security in an organization," says Peter Vincent, a security architect at IBM, in a video by Inspired Careers.

Many people who end up as information security architects do not follow such a straight path. Since every industry needs security professionals, it is possible for someone who starts out in any field—say as a pharmacist, bank teller, or project manager—to begin to dabble in information security through getting involved in work projects related to security or taking courses online or at a community college. That person will bring valuable knowledge of the health care industry, finance, business, or another field to his or her work in information security. In an article on TechRepublic, Shelley Westman, a senior vice president at the security software company Protegrity says, "It's a myth in the industry that you have to be technical to be in the field of cyber." Westman started her career as a lawyer. "We need people who have deep analytical skills, who can talk to clients, and translate technical speak to business value."

What Is the Future Outlook for Information Security Architects?

Demand for talent in cybersecurity has skyrocketed in recent years. Experts predict that by 2022, 1.8 million jobs in the field will go unfilled, according to the 2017 Global Information Security Workforce Study. Openings for information security analysts and engineers are most plentiful, but companies are also having trouble finding architects and other senior-level talent. When people with the right skill set are not available, companies may settle for applicants with less experience and provide on-the-job training or reimbursement for outside courses. David Dumas told the author, "I'm telling people just trying to get into the field that it's one of the fastest growing fields right now. Every single company has computers and has a network, and has something someone else wants to steal from them." That means that every single company needs information security architects to protect their assets.

Find Out More

Information Systems Security Association (ISSA)
1964 Gallows Rd., Suite 310
Vienna, VA 22182
website: www.issa.org

The ISSA is an international community devoted to helping cybersecurity professionals advance in their careers. The group organizes conferences, meet-ups, and other events for security professionals.

International Information System Security
Certification Consortium (ISC)^2
311 Park Place Blvd., Suite 400
Clearwater, FL 33759
website: www.isc2.org

This professional organization helps information security professionals learn, grow, and thrive. (ISC)^2 provides the CSSLP certification as well as other forms of education and training.

ISACA
3701 Algonquin Rd., Suite 1010
Rolling Meadows, IL 60008
website: www.isaca.org

Formerly known as the Information Systems Audit and Control Association, this organization sponsors the development and adoption of best practices for information systems. This group offers the well-respected CISM certification as well as more general training.

SANS Institute
11200 Rockville Pike, Suite 200
North Bethesda, MD 20852
website: www.sans.org

This organization facilitates the sharing of important information and research among information security professionals. It also operates the Internet Storm Center, a free service that monitors the public Internet for malicious attacks.

Ethical Hacker

What Does an Ethical Hacker Do?

Ethical hackers get paid to think and act like criminal hackers. They try to break into real computer systems, except they do not actually steal or harm anything. Instead, they help the people in charge of the system understand how to prevent or respond to similar attacks in the future.

Ethical hackers go by many names, including penetration testers, white hat hackers, or red team testers. The term *red team* comes from the military. In traditional exercises to prepare for a real combat scenario, a red team practices attacking something while a blue team defends. Similarly, a group of ethical hackers performs a red team test to simulate a real cyberattack. The hackers usually try to steal specific data or gain access to specific systems through any means necessary. Penetration testing is much more common and generalized than a red team test. In penetration testing, the goal is to find and define as many potential security issues as possible.

Ethical hackers do not have to play fair. They may use whatever tactics a criminal hacker might try in order to get past security measures. Using programming tricks or malicious computer code to get

At a Glance

Ethical Hacker

Minimum Educational Requirements
Varies; may be self-taught

Personal Qualities
Strong analytical and communication skills, creativity

Certification and Licensing
CEH, OSCP, GPEN, and more

Working Conditions
Typically contract-based work

Average Salary
Around $95,155

Number of Jobs
Around 6,695 online job postings per year as of 2017*

* This number comes from postings for penetration testers, a very similar job.

into a system is not the only way. Sometimes they trick employees into willingly handing over access. For example, a hacker might find out who is on vacation, then call a coworker explaining that the person who is away had promised access to sensitive files. The coworker probably wants to be helpful and may not think to check the caller's identity. This kind of approach to hacking is called social engineering.

Ben Miller, an ethical hacker at the company Parameter Security, talks about his job in a Career Spotlight interview on the *Lifehacker* blog. He says:

> People in this profession use all sorts of tricks to sneak in—you can hack your way in, con employees over the phone or email, use impersonation to walk in, it really doesn't matter. I've never come across a business that couldn't be compromised. I've broken into a wide range of companies and organizations, from banks to hospitals, Fortune 500s, manufacturers, city utilities, government agencies, you name it.

Before a red team or penetration test, ethical hackers must learn as much as they can about the client's business and security measures. They need to figure out what an attacker might want to target. After a test is over, ethical hackers must document everything that happened in a report to the client. They also provide recommendations for how to move forward. "Much of my time is spent probing or scanning networks, looking for vulnerabilities, etc., but just as much time is spent communicating with the client and documenting what I've done in a written report," says Miller. Reports help the client understand the most important steps to take to improve security and also how to limit the damage in a real attack scenario. "The ultimate objective is helping customers understand their risk and helping them secure their data," says John Yeo, director of SpiderLabs for Europe, the Middle East, and Africa at Trustwave, in an article on the website Help Net Security. "Being a technically gifted and committed penetration tester is only part of the journey."

How Do You Become an Ethical Hacker?

Education

In general, experience matters much more than education in a career as an ethical hacker. Hackers must break and fix computer code and computer systems, again and again. This is not a job that a person can expect to begin right out of school. Students interested in this job should focus on developing technical skills and security skills while in school to prepare for a first job as an information technology (IT) professional or software developer.

For the best chance of success as an ethical hacker, a student should get a bachelor's degree in computer science, computer engineering, or IT. Going on to earn a master's degree in information security will only enhance a student's chances of success. However, a two-year associate's degree in IT that leads to steady work in IT may provide a strong enough foundation. An alternate path is to join the military and focus on IT or intelligence. This path can lead to ethical hacker jobs for the government or military organizations that require special clearance to access and protect classified information.

Certification and Licensing

While certifications are not required to work as an ethical hacker, any information security certification will set a person apart and help prove his or her commitment to the field. The Certified Ethical Hacker (CEH) certification is designed specifically for this type of work. To get the CEH certification, an individual must attend a training course or provide evidence of two years of work experience in information security, then pass an exam. The Offensive Security Certified Professional (OSCP) and GIAC Penetration Tester (GPEN) are two more certifications that focus on ethical hacking.

Internships and Hacking Competitions

Internships are an excellent way to begin any information security career. It may be difficult or impossible to find an internship specifically focused on ethical hacking, but one that provides IT or information security experience can prove just as valuable. The key is to get real-world experience in how computer systems and networks function and how they might be compromised.

It is important for someone interested in a career as an ethical hacker not to practice breaking into real systems. Even if the hacker does not intend to steal anything, the breach may cause serious trouble or even lead to jail time. Hacking competitions can help provide the experience an ethical hacker needs in a safe environment. The Global CyberLympics pits teams of college students and security professionals against each other in ethical hacking challenges. Other organizations, including r00tz Asylum, offer similar hacking competitions for kids and teens. These events are a great way to develop technical and social hacking skills without doing anything illegal.

Skills and Personality

To many people interested in cybersecurity, working as an ethical hacker seems like a dream job. While it can be exhilarating to play a criminal, the work is also very challenging. Ethical hackers must develop and maintain extremely strong technical skills, especially in networking and network devices, databases, and programming languages, such as C, LISP, Perl, and Java. They must master the same technologies, tools, and techniques that criminal hackers are using. These change and evolve rapidly as criminals continually try new ways to get past security. Ethical hackers must study and learn from new cyberattacks as they occur. And they must think more smartly and creatively than the "bad guys" in order to help the "good guys" stay a few steps ahead. At the same time, they must develop strong communication skills in order to keep their clients well informed.

Criminal and ethical hackers tend to have similar personalities. Their excellent communication skills also allow them to use social engineering. They are master problem solvers who thrive in intense, fast-paced situations. They often feel a thrill when they outsmart a system. What separates ethical hackers from criminals is a desire to protect people and their data. An ethical hacker does not hurt or exploit others.

On the Job

Employers

Most ethical hackers work at consulting companies that provide penetration testing or red team testing services to clients in a variety of industries. Ethical hackers may also work freelance, and they often start out doing the work as a side project while working full time in another position. The companies HackerOne and Bugcrowd connect freelance hackers to companies willing to pay people who find vulnerabilities in their software or applications (apps). These are called "bug-bounty" programs.

The industries with the greatest need for ethical hacking are those that protect the most sensitive data; for example, health care and financial businesses. As cyberwarfare and cyberterrorism become greater threats, many government agencies and militaries are hiring or working with ethical hackers. The US government is a top employer of ethical hackers, and Washington, DC, is a hub for this type of work.

Working Conditions

Since most ethical hackers work as consultants, they take work on a contract basis. A series of test attacks for one client may last two to ten weeks. During that time, each hacker on a team will likely work eight- to ten-hour days during normal business hours. In between jobs, ethical hackers write reports for current clients and look for new clients. Those who work freelance set their own hours.

In a red team test, ethical hackers may work alongside other specialists. A red team may include a mission planner, an expert in physical break-ins, as well as hackers who specialize in communications or IT. The team may also include experts in social engineering.

Earnings

An ethical hacker's earnings vary depending on the person's experience and employer. It can be difficult to make a living as a freelance hacker completing bug-bounty projects. Though

Google pays up to $20,000 for a single bug, most rewards are much smaller. "You could do research for hours, then get paid 50 or 100 bucks or so," says Clifford Trigo, a freelance ethical hacker who lives in the Philippines, in an article in the *Atlantic*. It may be more sustainable to work at a consulting firm or for the government or military. Ethical hackers who work full time tend to earn excellent salaries. Professionals with the CEH certification earn an average of $95,155 per year.

Opportunities for Advancement

Most people working as ethical hackers are already midway through their careers. Many start out in IT positions then move on to become information security analysts. While working as an analyst, they focus on gaining experience in penetration testing. Finally, after at least two years of experience, a professional can qualify for an ethical hacker certification and start to look for work as an ethical hacker.

To move up in the field, an ethical hacker may choose to specialize in a certain area. For example, the hacker may perfect the art of social engineering or may become an expert at breaking into databases, mobile or web apps, or industrial control systems at utilities or factories. An ethical hacker who learns management skills may become a team leader. With enough experience, an ethical hacker may work as an independent consultant or may run his or her own consulting company.

What Is the Future Outlook for Ethical Hackers?

Ethical hacking work is very specialized. As of 2017, only around 6,695 jobs for ethical hackers get posted online in the United States each year. Jobs for information security analysts, engineers, and architects are much more plentiful, with hundreds of thousands of openings. Often, people in these more general roles also perform penetration testing or ethical hacking as part of their usual duties.

In the future, demand for all information security work, including ethical hacking, will grow at a fast pace. The industry must grow in order to keep up with cyberattacks as they increase in number, scope, and severity. "Hackers are part of the immune system for the technology age," said Keren Elazari during a 2016 keynote speech at an International Association of Privacy Professionals conference in London. In 2015 the US director of national intelligence published a report that listed cyberattacks over terrorism and weapons of mass destruction as the world's number one threat. To counter this threat, the world needs more hackers who use their skills for good.

Find Out More

CyberPatriot: The National Youth Cyber Education Program
1501 Lee Hwy.
Arlington, VA 22209
website: www.uscyberpatriot.org

The Air Force Association started the CyberPatriot program to inspire students toward careers in cybersecurity and other related fields. The program's offerings include an annual competition, cyber camps, and elementary education activities.

DEF CON
website: www.defcon.org

Hacking competitions, also known as Capture the Flag events, are a great way to hone skills as an ethical hacker. DEF CON is one of the oldest and most prestigious events for hackers. It is a conference that offers information and networking opportunities for hackers as well as competitions, including the r00tz Asylum competition for kids and teens.

EC-Council
EC-Council New Mexico
101C Sun Ave. NE
Albuquerque, NM 87109
website: www.eccouncil.org

The EC-Council is a professional organization that supports people working in information security, especially those focused on disaster recovery, ethical hacking, and forensic investigation. The EC-Council offers many certifications, including Certified Ethical Hacker.

Offensive Security
website: www.offensive-security.com

Offensive Security is a company that teaches students methods for penetration testing in a safe environment. It offers the Offensive Security Certified Professional certification.

picoCTF
Carnegie Mellon University
Information Networking Institute
College of Engineering
4616 Henry St.
Pittsburgh, PA 15213
website: http://picoctf.com

Sponsored by Carnegie Mellon University, picoCTF is a computer security game for middle and high school students. The game consists of a series of challenges all set up with the intent of being hacked, making it an excellent, legal way to get hands-on experience reverse engineering, breaking, decrypting, and hacking.

Cyber Incident Responder

What Does a Cyber Incident Responder Do?

Cyber incident responders are the firefighters of the digital world. Information security analysts and architects will not always succeed in preventing cyberattacks. So when an incident occurs, responders rush to the scene to fight back. However, cyberattacks are not as obvious as a fire. A company's sensitive data may get stolen without anyone realizing anything happened. So one of the most important responsibilities for cyber incident responders is detecting signs of an attack. If a breach is underway, they work to boot attackers out of the system. If damage has already occurred, they investigate what happened and make repairs. Some incident responders specialize in malware or virus analysis. This job involves reverse engineering a dangerous computer program in order to create defenses against it. People working in this role are also known as security incident analysts or handlers, intrusion detection specialists, or network intrusion analysts.

At a Glance

Cyber Incident Responder

Minimum Educational Requirements
Associate's degree

Personal Qualities
Confidence and adaptability, thrives under pressure, excellent communication skills

Certification and Licensing
GCIH, CND, and more

Working Conditions
May work twenty-four-hour shifts when responding to an incident

Salary Range
Around $48,707 to $105,330

Number of Jobs
Around 14,550 online job postings per year as of 2017

33

Rob Sherman is director of incident management at Flowers Foods, a company that produces packaged baked goods. Before becoming a cyber incident responder, he worked as a firefighter. "A fire fighter's main duty is to protect," he says in an article on the security news website CSO. "Protecting to a fire fighter may be teaching fire safety, or training, or learning new tools. The same can be said with incident response. . . . Thinking on your feet, using tools, having an incident commander, and bringing in the right response in a timely fashion all fall within incident response."

Cyber incident responders are often responsible for leading a defensive "blue team." This is a military term that refers to the group that works to defend against the enemy during a training exercise. O'Shea Bowens is an information security consultant and founder of Null Hat Security, a company that focuses on incident response. In a conversation with the author, he explained that his blue team exercises involve getting the individuals on a company's security team together in a room and running through attack scenarios with them. "I'm watching how they respond, how they communicate with each other," says Bowens. His blue team exercises assess the skill level and knowledge of a company's security team. He looks for any gaps in the company's process or in the coverage of the security tools it is using. He explains that it is not enough for a company to have expensive security tools. "They also have to actively deploy those tools . . . to verify how they stand up against an attack," he says. After a blue team exercise, a cyber incident responder will make a plan for how to improve the team's skills and the company's defenses moving forward.

When a real cyberattack occurs, cyber incident responders often help reconstruct what happened. This part of the job involves digital forensics, or gathering evidence from computer systems. Digital forensics investigators or members of law enforcement may need to get involved. Incident responders work with these professionals to look carefully at network traffic and log data to try to determine when and where the attack occurred. They must also track down any lost data. For example, an attacker may hide sensitive information within an image file in order to get it past a data loss prevention system. The attacker may also delete data, so incident responders need to know how to identify and recover deleted files. They must carefully copy and track all evidence they gather in case it ends up becoming part of a legal case. Meanwhile, they must keep upper management, the public relations team, the legal team, and other key stakeholders informed on the breadth and depth of the incident.

How Do You Become a Cyber Incident Responder?

Education

Most entry-level cyber incident response positions require at least an associate's degree in information technology (IT) or computer science, plus some work experience in IT. It will be even easier to get a job with a bachelor's degree in either field. A master's degree in information security or information assurance is not required, but it could lead to higher pay or management-level positions.

John Meyers works as an incident response and forensic specialist for the computer company Hewlett Packard. He talks about his education in the book *Breaking into Information Security: Crafting a Custom Career Path to Get the Job You Really Want*. He attended a local community college, where he enrolled in the associate's degree program in Information Systems, Network & PC. While in school, he worked part time in the college's IT department. During that time, he became interested in information security and began taking courses through the SANS Institute, an organization that provides information security training and certifications. "Basically, I tried to learn skills that would lead to some kind of Incident Handler job," he says in the book. The training paid off when he got his dream job at Hewlett Packard.

Certification and Licensing

Cyber incident responders do not need to have certifications. However, many employers look for these credentials when hiring. Certified Network Defender (CND) and GIAC Certified Incident Handler (GCIH) are both targeted toward this particular role in cybersecurity. Other, more general cybersecurity certifications are helpful as well. Tenisha Mitchell works as an information assurance specialist at the Defense Advanced Research Projects Agency, a US research agency, and holds a Certified Information Systems Security Professional (CISSP) certification. In a video by the International Information System Security Certification Consortium, the organization that provides the certification, she says, "The agency that I work for currently is a prestigious agency that's known worldwide. I don't think I would have landed the role without the CISSP certification." Positions for government agencies may also require special security clearance in order to access and protect classified information.

Internships and Mentors

Certifications look good on a résumé, but often they do not adequately prepare a person for the reality of working in security. Experience handling actual security incidents is key in becoming a talented cyber incident responder. Though it may not be possible to find an internship in incident response, since this is a very specialized field, an information security analyst internship would offer the opportunity to learn about the defensive side of security. Mentors are also extremely important. Sherman explains that his mentor "taught me how to think differently, and to really have a strong work ethic."

Skills and Personality

An incident responder must develop strong technical skills. A person in this role must thoroughly understand network protocols, applications, and services as well as security concepts, including confidentiality, authentication, access control and privacy, malware and viruses, and various security vulnerabilities. Programming skills are a plus but not required.

When it comes to personality, cyber incident responders must be able to remain calm and continue working steadily during a tense emergency situation. They must not freeze or panic. As the firefighters of the digital world, they must dive in and save as much data as they can. "If you falter at the first sign of a chal-

A cyber incident responder might bring members of a company's security team together for training exercises. He or she will run them through various attack scenarios and then assess their performance.

lenge, you're likely not going to perform well in a blue team scenario," Bowens told the author.

Excellent communication skills are also important. Cyber incident responders must be able to explain the details of an attack to nontechnical people. They may also have to communicate directly with the attacker or attackers. Since attackers may come from anywhere in the world, knowledge of foreign languages comes in handy in these situations.

On the Job

Employers

The majority of cyber incident responders work for technology or IT companies. Some of these companies provide security consulting services for prevention before an attack or for cleanup afterward. In the CSO article, Debbie Henley, president of the information security recruitment firm Redbud, says "about 65 percent of incident response management is handled in house."

Other industries that employ the most cyber incident responders are banking, education, health care, and the government. Regardless of the industry or number of employees, all companies need to be able to respond to cybersecurity incidents. A 2014 survey by the SANS Institute of professionals working in incident response found an even spread of respondents working at companies with fewer than one hundred employees all the way up to over twenty thousand employees. Whatever the size of the company, Sherman recommends that cyber incident responders focus on finding a place to work where the security team will receive the support it needs. "If the leadership of the organization does not have a focus on security, it becomes an uphill battle from the start," he says.

Working Conditions

Cyber incident responders typically work in shifts at a security operations center, also known as an SOC. This schedule ensures security coverage at all times. However, the SOC does not face major cyberattacks every day. At many companies, no one bears the job title of cyber incident responder. Instead, information security analysts or engineers take on additional responsibility as members of a designated computer security incident response team (CSIRT). This is a group of staff members responsible for coordinating the response to a cyberattack. In addition to cybersecurity experts, the team includes management, IT, attorneys, auditors, and human resources and public relations personnel. Law enforcement and technical specialists may need to get involved as well.

When a CSIRT is responding to an incident, the people on the team will have to work long hours in a stressful environment. "That's when you're in crisis mode and you can easily pull a few all-nighters trying to stop the attack from progressing, control the damage, and figure out how to get the company back on track," Ben Miller, an ethical hacker who has also worked in incident response, says in an interview on the *Lifehacker* blog. Incident responders typically get flex time to make up for such a grueling period. They may work two twenty-four-hour shifts and then get the rest of the week off.

Earnings

A cyber incident responder's compensation depends on his or her education and work experience. The average salary falls between $48,707 and $105,330, with a median of $70,388, according to salary and compensation information provider PayScale. Those with associate's degrees will typically earn less than those who have earned a bachelor's or master's degree.

Opportunities for Advancement

As with other information security specialties, cyber incident responders typically start off in entry-level IT positions then advance to become security analysts or incident responders within a few years. After around five years of experience in cyber incident response, the career path hits a crossroads. Most people have to choose between focusing on moving into a management role or remaining in a more junior role, where they will be able to use and grow their technical expertise, explains Bowens. Management duties include running an SOC or leading a CSIRT. This path ends at the highest possible position in information security, chief information security officer. Those who prefer more technical work typically advance to become senior or principal security incident responders. Or they may move sideways into positions as security engineers or architects. Bowens took a less common path. He decided to start his own consulting company focused on incident response. "I thought, why not branch out on my own? I will still be responsible for the technical side of incident response, but will also be able to manage my own operation and work with different clients."

What Is the Future Outlook for Incident Responders?

Every business and organization in the world that uses computers and the Internet needs personnel who can respond to a cyberattack. "The demand for cyber security incident responders remains high," says Henley. Her company, Redbud, helps companies fill cybersecurity jobs. She says that two out of three placements her company makes are related to incident response. Worldwide, there will be 3.5 million unfilled cybersecurity jobs by 2021, according to a report from Cybersecurity Ventures, an industry analyst. "Incident responders [are] a big part of that. The shortage is staggering," says Henley. People who specialize in cyber incident response should have no trouble finding work.

Find Out More

CSO from IDG
492 Old Connecticut Path
PO Box 9208
Framingham, MA 01701
website: www.csoonline.com

CSO is a website that provides news and information targeted toward security professionals. Its content addresses risk management, network defense, fraud, data loss prevention, and more.

EC-Council
EC-Council New Mexico
101C Sun Ave. NE
Albuquerque, NM 87109
website: www.eccouncil.org

The EC-Council is a professional organization that supports people working in information security, especially those focused on disaster recovery, ethical hacking, and forensic investigation. The EC-Council offers many certifications, including Certified Network Defender.

Forum of Incident Response and Security Teams (FIRST)
PO Box 1187
Morrisville, NC 27560
website: www.first.org

FIRST is a forum that security incident response teams use to share experiences, tips, and other information. The organization also hosts conferences and meetings.

International Information System Security
Certification Consortium (ISC)^2
311 Park Place Blvd., Suite 400
Clearwater, FL 33759
website: www.isc2.org

This professional organization helps information security professionals learn, grow, and thrive. (ISC)^2 provides the well-respected CISSP certification as well as other forms of education and training.

SANS Institute
11200 Rockville Pike, Suite 200
North Bethesda, MD 20852
website: www.sans.org

This organization facilitates the sharing of important information and research among information security professionals. It also operates the Internet Storm Center, a free service that monitors the public Internet for malicious attacks.

Digital Forensics Investigator

At a Glance

Digital Forensics Investigator

Minimum Educational Requirements
Bachelor's degree

Personal Qualities
A passion for justice, attention to detail

Certification and Licensing
GCFA, GCFE, CHFI, and more

Working Conditions
Often requires travel and court appearances

Salary Range
Around $42,927 to $114,750

Number of Jobs
Around 15,400 in the United States as of 2016*

Future Job Outlook
Growth of 17 percent through 2026*

* Numbers come from the Bureau of Labor Statistics listing for forensic science technicians, a category that includes digital forensics investigators.

What Does a Digital Forensics Investigator Do?

A digital forensics investigator is a detective who solves crimes that involve computers, the Internet, or mobile devices. "It's kind of like *CSI* but with computers," says Chris Kimmel, referring to the popular TV drama. Kimmel earned his degree in digital forensics and talked about the work in a video by the Career Zoo. Other titles for this role include forensic computer examiner or computer forensics analyst, specialist, or technician. This job links two separate industries: criminal justice and cybersecurity.

On the criminal justice side, digital forensics investigators belong to a larger category of forensic science technicians, or people who analyze evidence in order to help solve a crime. In cybersecurity, the job overlaps with the role of cyber incident responder, as these first responders often help gather evidence during and after a cyberattack.

A digital forensics investigator's job begins when a crime involving digital media is identified. Digital crimes include everything from electronic fraud, scams, and identity theft to cyberterrorism and the distribution of illegal pornography. The investigator must gain access to the computers or other devices that were involved in the crime. While gathering evidence from these devices, a digital forensics investigator must follow strict standards in order to ensure that the evidence is correct and complete. For example, investigators make a digital copy of a computer or mobile phone, then attempt to recover deleted files from the copy. Creating a copy leaves the original evidence unaltered. An investigator may also have to repair or rebuild damaged devices in order to access the evidence.

Digital forensics investigators must write reports of the evidence they recover. "Much of your day will be spent in documentation," says John Irvine, vice president at the data recovery and digital forensics company CyTech Services, in an interview on the Balance Careers website. "You might be writing a report of analysis, peer reviewing another examiner's report, or noting everything you did when performing an exam."

If a case goes to court, digital forensics investigators may be called to testify. Evidence they discover helps put guilty people behind bars or helps innocent people go free. Mark Johnson started out as a police officer and eventually established a computer forensics division at his department. Now he is a computer forensic analyst for the US Department of Justice in Kansas City, Missouri. In a video by the Parkway Alumni Association, Johnson says, "If there's a crime with a computer involved in it, it will come to us. We can find the deleted information, the hidden information, do timeline analysis, all in trying to put a good case together for the prosecutor."

Sometimes, the outcome of the work is very positive. "The single best result of the work . . . is finding a missing child," says André DiMino in an interview on EngineerJobs.com. DiMino is a computer forensic information security systems engineer who has worked on investigations. He says, "You are responsible . . . to piece together all the disparate bits of information across a computer, or several, to discover where [the child] might be." The worst part of the job, in his opinion, is deciding which cases are most important and which have to wait. On crime shows like *CSI*, data analysis tends to take seconds. But in reality, it often takes days or weeks to properly and completely analyze evidence. The job of a digital forensics investigator is not as dramatic or exciting as a show like *CSI* makes it seem. But it is certainly an important role that helps deliver justice and keep society safe.

How Do You Become a Digital Forensics Investigator?

Education

Earning a bachelor's degree in digital forensics is the best way to launch a career in this field. Course work for the degree will include classes on computer networks, programming, criminal law, mobile device forensics, and more. However, this is not the only way to get started as a digital forensics investigator. The job combines two different skill sets: technical computer knowledge and law enforcement. So an education in either of those areas will help a person prepare for this job. For example, a bachelor's degree in information technology (IT), computer science, or engineering builds strong technical and problem-solving skills. DiMino got his degree in electrical engineering. He says, "Engineering especially prepares someone to be a good forensic examiner. It makes you be detail-oriented . . . it teaches you how to think and not to take things at face value."

Other people start out in law enforcement. Becoming a police officer only requires a high school diploma, but candidates must go through rigorous training at a police academy. An associate's degree in forensic science prepares a person for entry-level work as an assistant or technician who gathers evidence from a crime scene. With additional training in computer science or IT, police officers and crime scene technicians can transition into digital forensics.

Certification and Licensing

Certifications are very important to success in this field. Numerous certifications exist that focus on digital forensics. The two most popular with employers are GIAC Certified Forensic Analyst (GCFA), which focuses more on information security and incident response, and GIAC Certified Forensic Examiner (GCFE), which focuses more on law enforcement. The EC-Council's Computer Hacking Forensic Investigator (CHFI) is also a well-respected certification.

Depending on the geographical area where a digital forensics investigator works, he or she may need to obtain a private investigator license. In the United States, Texas, Michigan, and Georgia all require licensure. In the United Kingdom, a license is not required. The rules about licensing for this type of work are still under debate, as it is not clear whether digital investigation belongs under the same license as other types of investigation.

Internships and Mentors

Education and certification cannot entirely prepare a person to work on real criminal cases. Irvine says, "Schools can give you a great foundation, but case experience helps you put people behind bars." Internships are one way to get real-world experience. The FBI offers an unpaid internship program and is specifically seeking people pursuing an education in cybersecurity or digital forensics. Internships in digital forensics are also available at many local justice departments as well as at some private companies and organizations. An internship is a great way to discover a mentor, or a person who can offer career guidance and support. Irvine stresses the importance of finding a mentor. "Computer Forensics is an apprenticeship discipline," he says. "You really learn the trade once you're in a seat working on real cases alongside a senior examiner."

Skills and Personality

Success in this field requires a passion for justice. Though technical skills are essential, it is the drive to solve cases that keeps most digital forensics investigators going. Irvine, who used to work for the FBI, says, "I've had significantly better luck training investigators in the technical details of the job than I've had

Digital forensics investigators gather evidence on digital crimes ranging from fraud to cyberterrorism. Sometimes the only way to gain access to evidence is to repair or rebuild damaged devices.

in teaching programmers methods of investigation and the art of 'the hunch.'" Putting a case together is like solving a puzzle. Careful, methodical work is required in order to get to the truth. The field also requires a very strong sense of personal responsibility. "You need to be willing to put your name and reputation on the line with each case you analyze, because you could very well end up in court based on the contents of your report," says Irvine. The job also requires taking the initiative to keep learning in order to keep up with the ever-changing nature of cybercrime.

On the Job

Employers

Many digital forensics investigators work in law enforcement. In the United States the government is one of the biggest employers. The CIA and FBI both actively seek agents with digital forensics and information security skills. Investigators also work for the governments of other countries and for state and city law enforcement agencies and justice departments. Alternatively, investigators can find work with private companies and organizations. Many information security consulting companies provide investigation services.

Working Conditions

Usually, digital forensics investigators can collect and transfer evidence electronically. So for the most part, they work in an office or crime laboratory during normal business hours, though they may need to put in extra hours while working on a case. When necessary, they testify in court. Travel may also be required, especially for those who work as consultants. "At any one point in time I can be involved in a number of investigations across a number of countries working with various clients," says computer forensic consultant Aaron Watson in an interview on KLDiscovery's blog. The job offers a lot of variety.

However, the work can also be emotionally taxing. Irvine points out that one of the most common computer crimes is the distribution of illegal pornography. Digital forensics investigators may also assist on murder, rape, or terrorism cases that involve mobile devices. Exposure to extremely disturbing images, videos, and text conversations is part of the job. "Many people who enter the field don't last," says Irvine. "On average, I'd say about fifty percent of the people who get into it leave within about two years." Those who stay develop a thick skin. On the positive side, the job offers great satisfaction in that investigators are responsible for helping maintain public safety.

Earnings

Digital forensics investigators earn from $42,927 to $114,750 per year, with a median salary of $69,100. Those who work as contractors for private investigative firms may earn as much as $200 to $400 per hour. On average, these specialists tend to make more than other forensic scientists, due to the highly technical nature of the work. Those who work as contractors have the potential to make the most, followed by investigators employed by the federal government, state governments, and the military. Those working for local governments tend to make the least.

Opportunities for Advancement

In law enforcement, entry-level digital forensics investigators work under the close supervision of a senior or lead investigator. Over time, entry-level professionals transition into lead roles and take responsibility for training the next generation. A person who starts out at a local or state law enforcement agency may advance to work for higher levels of the government. In the United States this includes jobs at the CIA or FBI. Often these job opportunities require security clearance because the investigator will need access to classified information. In a private business or organization, digital forensics investigators often transition into management roles or other areas of information security, particularly incident response. The highest possible role at a private company is that of chief information security officer.

What Is the Future Outlook for Digital Forensics Investigators?

For anyone who has ever dreamed of becoming a special agent, detective, or investigator, digital forensics is an excellent choice. The technical skills required to gather evidence from digital media are in high demand. In 2014 and 2015 the FBI ran an advertising campaign that aimed to attract cybersecurity experts to work as agents. In an article for the campaign, Robert Anderson Jr., executive assistant director for the FBI's Criminal, Cyber, Response, and Services Branch, said, "We're looking to hire a lot of cyber agents now. It's an area where the FBI and the whole U.S. government will be looking for this talent for years to come." Cybercrime is everywhere these days. Investigative entities are struggling to find enough people with the skills to solve these cases and reduce the overall threat of cyberattacks.

Find Out More

CyberPatriot: The National Youth Cyber Education Program
1501 Lee Hwy.
Arlington, VA 22209
website: www.uscyberpatriot.org

The Air Force Association started the CyberPatriot program to inspire students toward careers in cybersecurity and other related fields. Its offerings include an annual competition, cyber camps, and elementary education activities.

EC-Council
EC-Council New Mexico
101C Sun Ave. NE
Albuquerque, NM 87109
website: www.eccouncil.org

The EC-Council is a professional organization that supports people working in information security, especially those focused on disaster recovery, ethical hacking, and forensic investigation. The EC-Council offers many certifications, including Computer Hacking Forensic Investigator.

International Association of Computer Investigative Specialists
5703 Fourth Ave., #3192
Ferndale, WA 98248
website: www.iacis.com

This nonprofit organization is dedicated to training digital forensics professionals around the world. It offers the Certified Forensic Computer Examiner certification.

International Society of Forensic Computer Examiners
9005 Overlook Blvd.
Brentwood, TN 37027
website: www.isfce.com

This organization provides the Certified Computer Examiner certification and also conducts research into new and emerging technologies and methods in digital forensics.

Data Privacy Attorney

Data Privacy Attorney

Minimum Educational Requirements
Juris doctor (law degree)

Personal Qualities
An analytical mind, strong ethics, excellent communication skills

Certification and Licensing
Must pass the bar examination

Working Conditions
High-pressure work, often more than forty hours per week

Salary Range
Around $57,430 to $208,000*

Number of Jobs
Around 792,500 in the United States as of 2016*

Future Job Outlook
Growth of 8 percent through 2026*

* Numbers come from the Bureau of Labor Statistics listing for lawyers, a category that includes data privacy attorneys.

What Does a Data Privacy Attorney Do?

A data privacy attorney is a lawyer who specializes in legal matters surrounding the storage and usage of personal information and other sensitive data. Every country has its own laws for how to properly handle data. In the United States the laws vary by state. A data privacy attorney is responsible for thoroughly understanding all laws that affect the clients or companies he or she works with. Some data privacy attorneys provide legal counsel on any issue pertaining to data or privacy. But others specialize in the privacy laws of a particular part of the world or a certain industry, usually health care, financial services, telecommunications, or education.

Each of these areas has its own compliance standards. For example, in the United States all health care providers must follow the Health Insurance Portability and Accountability Act of 1996. This law helps ensure that patients' sensitive health information remains private. In the European Union (EU), a new law called the General Data Protection Regulation became effective in May 2018. The law affects all companies, even ones in the United States, that handle personal data of EU citizens. In order to comply with the law, all major companies now have to encrypt all personal data, notify customers promptly when a breach has occurred, allow customers to delete their data, and more. Data privacy attorneys make sure their employers or clients keep their business practices in line with the law. "It's your responsibility to make sure everyone knows what [rules] they're supposed to be following," says attorney Kate Norris in an interview on the *Career Corner* podcast. "There are rules on just about everything! If I think there's not a rule for it, I'm probably wrong. It's somewhere and I've got to find it." Norris, who works as the compliance manager and privacy officer at the Emily Program, a mental health services provider, regularly receives e-mails asking whether a specific situation complies with the law. Her job is to do the legal research to find the answer. For example, one day she might read through the tasks that a nurse practitioner is allowed to perform in a particular state.

When a compliance issue occurs, data privacy attorneys help resolve the issue. In the case of a major data breach or cyberattack, these attorneys play an important role in incident response. They anticipate and handle any lawsuits or criminal cases that arise due to the incident. For example, if customers sue a company after a data breach, that company's attorneys might have to defend its interests in court. Even if attorneys do not have clients who are involved in the lawsuit, they may write reports called amicus briefs that provide the court with relevant background information.

Data privacy attorneys also assist companies and organizations with writing or revising privacy policies, customer agreements, and contracts related to confidentiality and security. Some work on product development to make sure privacy issues are addressed early in the design process. "You're really an advisor and consultant for the rest of the organization," notes Norris.

How Do You Become a Data Privacy Attorney?

Education

It takes at least seven years of higher education to become a lawyer. After earning a four-year bachelor's degree, the student must also complete three years of law school to earn a juris doctor degree. If privacy law is the goal, then a bachelor's degree in a technical field such as computer science or information technology is a great first step. However, a technical background is not required. Experts advise that those interested in law school should start out with a college major they find interesting.

Once accepted into law school, students should select some courses that focus on information privacy law, an area in which all law schools now offer classes. However, since this is a relatively new area of law, some schools may not offer very many classes. Students should also do their own research and find other ways to learn about the field.

Getting a law degree right out of college is not the only way to enter the field. A two-year or four-year degree in health information management or information assurance can get a person into a position as an information assurance specialist or privacy officer. People in these positions help ensure a company's compliance to privacy laws. Once in this type of position, earning a law degree would help advance the person's career to the next level.

Certification and Licensing

Lawyers must pass a rigorous test called the bar examination, or "the bar" for short, in order to practice law in a particular area. In the United States each state has its own bar examination. Those who pass become licensed to practice law in that state.

Additional optional certifications exist. The Certified Information Privacy Professional certification is an important credential for anyone working in the privacy business. As of 2018, lawyers who earn this certification may officially call themselves privacy law specialists.

Volunteer Work and Internships

Summer internships are an essential part of any lawyer's education. These positions offer practical experience working in a law firm or on a corporate legal team. Many law schools also offer externships or field placements. These allow students to earn academic credit while gaining work experience.

Volunteer work is another way to gain experience. "Consider serving as a volunteer advisor or board member helping a nonprofit gain insight into the world of privacy and data protection," suggests Peter A. Rabinowitz, who has served as chief privacy officer at PayPal and American Express, in an interview on the Kerwin Associates blog. Networking with a community of other lawyers and privacy professionals also helps lead to success. Online communities and professional organizations are a great source for connections, mentors, and advice.

Skills and Personality

Lawyers must regularly decide on the correct course of action in tricky situations. This skill requires excellent judgment and a strong sense of right and wrong, also called ethics. Communication skills are essential, as lawyers must be able to understand complex rules and regulations and communicate that understanding to others without legal backgrounds. Their speaking and writing must be clear, concise, and persuasive.

In the area of data privacy, it helps to have some technical skills. "Lawyers with backgrounds in technology are in high demand," writes George Washington University Law School professor Daniel Solove in an article for LinkedIn. "If you can code, you will be particularly in demand. And you don't even need to be a techie—just being well-versed enough to understand the issues is a big plus."

On the Job

Employers

Data privacy attorneys have several different options when it comes to employers. The first option is to work for a private law firm. These firms may be quite small, serving a single community, or they may be huge multinational businesses, such as Ropes & Gray, Bird & Bird, or Fieldfisher. In an article on the *Lawyer* website, Hazel Grant of Fieldfisher says that her firm is on the lookout for lawyers with data protection expertise. "Ideally I want someone who's got 100 per cent data protection experience," she says.

The second option is to become a public servant and work for the government. The regulatory agencies that make laws governing privacy issues, such as the Federal Trade Commission in the United States, need lawyers to help develop the laws and bring cases against those who break them. Finally, data privacy attorneys may seek employment at private companies or organizations. The industries with the most demand for in-house data privacy attorneys are the ones that are the most highly regulated: health care, financial services, telecommunications, and education.

Working Conditions

The legal profession has a reputation for fast-paced, intense, and stressful work. The amount of pressure a data privacy attorney will face on the job depends on the task at hand. When involved in incident response or a court case, the time pressure may be intense. In these situations, data privacy attorneys may work more than forty hours in a week and may have to travel or appear in court. However, when researching the law, drafting documentation or reports, or handling minor compliance issues, the work is typically much less demanding.

Earnings

Lawyers have the potential to earn excellent pay. However, salaries vary widely. While the top-paid 10 percent of the profession earn more than $208,000 per year, the lowest-paid 10 percent earn less than $57,430 yearly. The median annual wage for all lawyers in the United States in 2017 was $119,250. Data privacy attorneys are more in demand than many other lawyer specialties. So they tend to earn slightly higher compensation, with a median salary of $125,080, according to PayScale, a provider of salary and compensation information. Extremely successful attorneys who work for the wealthiest clients may earn $1 million or more in a year.

Opportunities for Advancement

The career path through a law firm is well defined. After completing law school, a person starts out as a junior associate, who works on projects under the close supervision of senior associates. Over the course of several years, a successful lawyer will earn the title of senior associate and will begin to manage his or her own projects. The eventual goal is to become a partner in the firm. Partners all share ownership of the business.

An attorney who works for a corporation may start as counsel and work his or her way up to senior counsel or general counsel. The general counsel is the highest attorney in a company or organization. A lawyer with data privacy experience may also find work in cybersecurity management. Shelley Westman got a law degree but wound up leaving that career to work in cybersecurity at IBM and later at Protegrity, a data security consulting company. She became senior vice president of Alliances & Field Operations there.

What Is the Future Outlook for Data Privacy Attorneys?

The Bureau of Labor Statistics predicts 8 percent growth in lawyer jobs through 2026, which is about the same as average for all occupations. For someone interested in a career as a lawyer, data privacy is one of the most lucrative areas to pursue. For new law school graduates in many US states, the competition for jobs has become brutal. Lawyers with data privacy experience, however, stand out from the crowd. "There is a huge interest in the area [of data protection]—everyone is hiring, both in-house and private practice," says Ruth Boardman of Bird & Bird in an article on the *Lawyer* website. The 2018 launch of the General Data Protection Regulation law in the EU will create new opportunities for data privacy attorneys in the United States and around the world, because all large companies must work to get in compliance.

Experts also predict that the emerging Internet of Things (IoT) will lead to higher demand for privacy regulations and a need for more data privacy lawyers. The IoT includes all products, such as clothing or appliances, that connect to the Internet and share data.

Find Out More

American Bar Association (ABA)
321 N. Clark St.
Chicago, IL 60654
website: www.americanbar.org

The ABA serves lawyers as one of the world's largest professional organizations, with over four hundred thousand members. Its goals include defending liberty and delivering justice as well as representing the legal profession.

Centre for Information Policy Leadership
2200 Pennsylvania Ave. NW
Washington, DC 20037
website: www.informationpolicycentre.com

This organization is a global privacy and security think tank that works with industry leaders and policy makers to develop best practices for privacy and data usage.

Future of Privacy Forum
1400 Eye St. NW, Suite 450
Washington, DC 20005
website: https://fpf.org

This nonprofit organization supports the development of principled data practices for emerging technologies for which laws have not yet been written.

International Association of Privacy Professionals
75 Rochester Ave., Suite 4
Portsmouth, NH 03801
website: https://iapp.org

This organization supports an international community of professionals working in the field of information privacy. Its goals are to help professionals advance their careers and to help organizations protect their data.

National Association for Law Placement
1220 Nineteenth St. NW, Suite 401
Washington, DC 20036
website: www.nalp.org

This organization advises and supports law students and lawyers through the hiring process. The group also provides standards for recruiting, professional and career development, and diversity and inclusion.

What Does a Security Auditor Do?

Security auditors determine if a company is handling information security the way it should. Like ethical hackers or penetration testers, they look for security vulnerabilities as well as gaps in an organization's policies and procedures. However, a security auditor is not trying to break into the company's systems. Instead, these professionals determine if the company is following industry standards and legal requirements. "The goal is to supply assurance that controls and protections are working the way people think they are working," Theresa Grafenstine, chair of the board at ISACA, a professional organization for information technology (IT) and security auditors, told the author. She points out that a lot of times, well-intentioned people believe that they are following all of the rules. But in practice, security controls may not be working as well as people think. Auditors provide a fresh set of eyes to find out what is really going on in day-to-day operations. "It's kind of like being a detective but through an IT lens," says Grafenstine.

At a Glance

Security Auditor

Minimum Educational Requirements
Bachelor's degree

Personal Qualities
Strong ethics, methodical and detail oriented, organized

Certification and Licensing
CISA, CRISC, ISO/IEC 27001 Lead Auditor, and more

Working Conditions
Office environment; travel may be required

Salary Range
Around $50,174 to $96,741

Number of Jobs
Around 6,663 online job postings per year as of 2017

Future Job Outlook
Growth of 10 percent through 2026*

* Number comes from the Bureau of Labor Statistics listing for accountants and auditors, a category that includes security auditors.

Every industry has its own set of best practices and standards for handling sensitive data. Some of these standards are voluntary, but others are required by law. For example, ISO/IEC 27001 is a voluntary certification that any company can acquire in order to reassure its customers that it is following the highest standards of information security. The Health Insurance Portability and Accountability Act of 1996, on the other hand, is a set of legal requirements for protecting patient health information in the United States. Auditors must thoroughly understand any government regulations or other standards that impact the companies they will be auditing.

Before performing an audit, a security auditor must spend time planning and preparing. Each business is a little different, so the auditor must strive to understand the standards this particular business hopes to follow and also the standards it must follow under the law. During the audit, these professionals work on teams. They talk to employees and perform tests on company networks, computers, and other devices. They often go through a long checklist of potential issues. Some items on the list are straightforward; for example, do employees sign out of their desktop computers before leaving their workstations? Other potential problems are much more technical. For example, can essential data and software be recovered after a disaster?

After completing the audit, security auditors prepare a report for the company's management team. The report highlights any information security areas in need of improvement or overhaul. And the audit process does not end here. Auditors typically follow up after a period of time to make sure that the company has corrected any problems covered in the report. Sailesh Halai works as an IT auditor and information security officer at the financial services company Redmayne-Bentley LLP. In an interview on the website IT Governance, he describes one challenge he faced during his career. "I had to get management to buy in to implementing an Information Security Management System that would be in line with ISO 27001 and at the same time meet the regulator's information security requirements. . . . I had to write new information security policies that the organization was missing."

How Do You Become a Security Auditor?

Education

A career as a security auditor begins with a bachelor's degree, typically in computer science, IT, information systems, business administration, or accounting. Some jobs, especially senior-level positions, may also require a master's degree in one of these fields or in information security. Halai got his bachelor's degree in computer studies and worked as an application developer before going back to school later in his career for a master's degree in computer systems auditing.

A computer science or IT degree focuses on how digital devices and networks function, while the other degrees are less technical. Information systems courses focus on the business implications of technology decisions, while accounting covers how to track and communicate financial transactions. A quarter of all security auditors hold accounting degrees, according to Sokanu, a career-matching platform. These professionals typically start out as financial auditors and transition into auditing for IT and security.

Certification and Licensing

Many security auditor positions require certification. Popular general certifications for this field include Certified Information Systems Auditor (CISA), GIAC Systems and Network Auditor, Certified in Risk and Information Systems Control (CRISC), Certified Internal Auditor, and Certified Fraud Examiner. Triona Bourke holds a CISA certification as an internal IT auditor at ICON plc, a medical research company. "I would strongly suggest any person within the audit space to take the CISA certification in order to develop a network but also to develop skills and knowledge within the area of audit and security," she says in a video by ISACA, the organization that provides the CISA. This certification applies to any general IT or security auditors. However, some auditors will also need to prove their knowledge of specific standards. The

To determine how secure a company's information is, security auditors often speak to employees. They also test company networks, computers, and other devices.

ISO/IEC 27001 Lead Auditor certification qualifies a person to lead an audit team that will help a company prove compliance to the ISO/IEC 27001 standards.

Volunteering and Internships

Many companies offer internships in IT auditing. These positions help students gain real-world experience in the job. Professional organizations can help prospective security auditors find internship opportunities and connect with others in the field. They also offer training and other resources. These organizations often need volunteers to help organize events. Grafenstine told the author that volunteering for ISACA "is the best thing I did as a young professional to get me on the path to where I'm at now."

Skills and Personality

An auditor is responsible for ensuring that a business follows rules and regulations. So it is vital that auditors believe that rules are important and essential to success. They should have a strong sense of right and wrong, also called ethics. In fact, CISA certification requires that auditors adhere to a professional code of ethics, which includes a promise to perform their duties objectively and to maintain the privacy and confidentiality of the information they audit.

Communication and interpersonal skills are both very important. The idea of an audit tends to make people uncomfortable, since they may fear that the process will reveal some wrongdoing. An ability to put people at ease helps immensely in this position. An auditor must also have the confidence to speak candidly with top executives and to give them bad news when necessary. Perseverance and resilience help a security auditor get through difficult situations. Tony Redlinger is senior manager for internal audit at the analytics company IHS Markit. In an interview with MISTI Training Institute, he says, "It's easy to get frustrated in this position because it's challenging, and the technology is always changing, but that's also what makes it so rewarding." He adds that auditors should strive to understand the systems they are testing. "Too often, we find ourselves with a check-the-box mentality without really understanding why we are checking the box or why it's important." Technical skills in computer science, IT, and information security all help provide a more thorough understanding.

On the Job

Employers

Most security auditors work for firms that companies hire to prove their compliance with information security or data privacy regulations. These external auditors act as impartial outsiders who take an objective look at a company's procedures. A group of international accounting firms nicknamed the Big Four all provide a range of professional services, including financial and security auditing. These four firms are Deloitte, PricewaterhouseCoopers,

Ernst & Young, and KPMG. Some external auditors work for government regulators. However, it is also possible to find work as an internal auditor. Some companies keep internal audit teams on staff to perform regular reviews of IT and security standards and procedures and keep upper management informed. Internal auditors tend to specialize in the information security rules and regulations of a particular industry, for example health care, financial services, education, or telecommunications.

Working Conditions

Auditing is an office job, but it involves a lot of face-to-face interaction. External auditors who work for one of the Big Four companies or another consulting firm gain a breadth of experience in a wide variety of industries. In this type of position, security auditors travel regularly, often to other countries. They meet new people at the offices of the companies they are auditing. Internal auditors have a more predictable schedule and tend to work in the same place with the same people every day. They may have the flexibility to work from home. However, both types of auditing can be demanding and stressful on occasion. "There may be times where your job will require you to put your personal life on hold," cautions Halai. "If you are not willing to make sacrifices, then perhaps a career in auditing is not the perfect match for you."

Earnings

Security auditors typically earn between $50,174 and $96,741 each year, with a median salary of $64,267, according to salary information provider PayScale. The position combines two very in-demand fields: accounting and information security. Grafenstine notes that having both of those backgrounds makes a person "super hirable." She told the author, "So few people have that skill set. If you get good at [IT security auditing], I promise you'll be able to get a job and negotiate to get a very good salary." Security auditors who pursue technical training, work for private companies, or go into consulting typically earn the highest salaries. Those working for nonprofit organizations or for the government tend to earn less.

Opportunities for Advancement

Many people who graduate with a business or accounting degree and have an interest in an auditing career look for an entry-level position at one of the Big Four companies. In these firms, a new hire starts out as an associate IT auditor. From there, he or she may gain enough experience and training to be promoted to senior IT auditor or lead IT auditor. The highest possible roles within these organizations are as a director or partner. Experience at one of the Big Four companies can provide an excellent jumping-off point to a job as an internal auditor in a specific industry, such as health care or telecommunications. That is because these large companies offer exposure to auditing in a variety of different industries around the world.

Experience in security or IT auditing in any industry can lead to positions in management; for example, as a data privacy officer. Government leadership positions may be available as well. Grafenstine worked as an IT security auditor for the government and eventually became the first female inspector general of the US House of Representatives. Some auditors who specialize in information security and data privacy may choose to leave auditing for a more technical career as an information security analyst, engineer, architect, or even as a chief information security officer.

What Is the Future Outlook for Security Auditors?

The Bureau of Labor Statistics predicts that jobs for all accountants and auditors will increase 10 percent through 2026, which is faster than the average for all occupations. IT and security auditing will likely grow at an even faster pace as countries around the world begin to enforce new guidelines and regulations regarding the proper protection of data. "There are huge opportunities for IT audit and advisory," says Rob Fijneman, a professor in IT auditing at Tilburg University, in an article for the IT advisory magazine *Compact*. He predicts that the continually evolving nature of new technology will trigger the need for companies to conduct ongoing IT audits. "Instead of performing these audits afterwards and fixing problems from the bottom up, we will be forced to act from the top down, ensuring the system is secure by design." He suggests that IT auditors will become ever more important partners in business decisions. In addition, security auditors who stay on top of new technology, including the Internet of Things, data analytics, artificial intelligence, and workflow automation, will find plentiful job opportunities.

Find Out More

Association of Certified Fraud Examiners
Gregor Building
716 West Ave.
Austin, TX 78701
website: www.acfe.com

This organization provides education and training with the goal of helping reduce business fraud worldwide. It provides the Certified Fraud Examiner certification.

Institute of Internal Auditors (IIA)
1035 Greenwood Blvd., Suite 401
Lake Mary, FL 32746
website: https://na.theiia.org

The IIA provides education and advocacy for professionals working in internal auditing, risk management, governance, internal control, IT auditing, education, and security.

International Organization for Standardization (ISO)
BIBC II
Chemin de Blandonnet 8
CP 401
1214 Vernier, Geneva
Switzerland
website: www.iso.org

The ISO is an independent, international organization that sets standards to help provide solutions to challenges facing the global community. These standards cover everything from technology and privacy to workplace safety, agriculture, and health care. The organization created the ISO/IEC 27001 standard, which provides requirements for information security management.

ISACA
3701 Algonquin Rd., Suite 1010
Rolling Meadows, IL 60008
website: www.isaca.org

This professional organization serves professionals working in governance, control, security, and audit positions. The group also sets standards, provides certifications, including the CISA, and runs industry publications and conferences.

MIS Training Institute
153 Cordaville Rd., Suite 200
Southborough, MA 01772
website: https://misti.com

This organization is an international leader in auditing, IT auditing, and information security training. The company provides courses to meet the needs of IT auditors and information security professionals.

Cryptologist

What Does a Cryptologist Do?

A cryptologist creates and breaks secret codes. This is the oldest information security profession, since coded messages have been around since ancient times. The earliest coded messages used scrambled letters or symbols and helped people exchange information in secret, usually during a war. Today coded messages have become an invisible part of daily life. To travel securely online, information must pass through encryption and decryption algorithms that employ advanced mathematical techniques to either convert text and data into unreadable code or to convert encoded text and data into readable form. A cryptologist must thoroughly understand these algorithms and the mathematical theories behind them in order to crack codes or develop new means of encryption.

Cryptology includes two related fields. Cryptography is the study of making codes, and cryptanalysis is the study of breaking them. A career in cryptology can go in several directions. Some cryptologists follow a purely academic route as cryptography researchers. They study methods of encryption and

At a Glance

Cryptologist

Minimum Educational Requirements
Varies

Personal Qualities
Love of puzzles, advanced math skills

Certification and Licensing
May need government security clearance

Working Conditions
Varies

Salary Range
Around $50,660 to $133,720*

Number of Jobs
Around 40,300 as of 2016*

Future Job Outlook
Growth of 33 percent through 2026, much faster than average*

* Numbers come from the Bureau of Labor Statistics listing for mathematicians, a category that includes cryptologists.

67

decryption and come up with new mathematical concepts and models. They typically publish papers on their findings and teach courses on the subject.

Other cryptologists apply these techniques in the real world. At private companies, they help make digital devices, transactions, or communications more secure using improved methods of encryption and decryption. They invent and apply new techniques to help protect personal information or authenticate messages and digital signatures. Some cryptologists specialize in cryptocurrency, a new form of money that relies on encryption and decryption. In an article on the *Times of India* website, Avishek Adhikari, a lecturer at the Department of Pure Mathematics at the University of Calcutta in India, says that cryptography helps protect anything that hackers may try to steal, from personal and medical data to mobile communications and state secrets. "To prevent such data theft, we need cryptographers to write stronger codes," he says. "In fact, currently, cryptography has broadened greatly from the study of secret writing to the study of information security."

Cryptologists also work for governments and militaries to assist with intelligence, commonly called spying. Common job titles for this type of work are cryptanalyst or cryptologic technician. In this role, cryptologists intercept and interpret enemy messages. Steve Barbee is a cryptologic technician interpretive (CTI) for the US Navy, specializing in Mandarin Chinese. Part of his job is to translate Chinese messages that the navy gathers, but he also has to figure out what the messages might imply. In a video by America's Navy, he says, "As a CTI, you learn everything there is to know about that culture or that region . . . in your day to day job a lot of times you're going to be called upon to read between the lines." The National Security Agency (NSA) in the United States also employs experts in this field. The details on what they do are classified. However, in an NSA Careers video, cryptanalyst Roger B. says that he feels his work directly impacts his country. "Sometimes in the blink of an eye a success you have can lead directly to intelligence that's going to support our US policy makers the next day," he says.

How Do You Become a Cryptologist?

Education

Educational requirements for cryptologists vary by industry. For a cryptology career in the US Navy, the highest degree required is a high school diploma. Any enlisted person who demonstrates an aptitude for math, languages, electronics, and technology may qualify to receive training to become a cryptologic technician. This training may include an all-expenses-paid college education or even graduate school. Service in other branches of the military or in the military in other countries may also help a person begin a career in cryptology as it relates to national intelligence.

For those not interested in military service, becoming a cryptologist requires a bachelor's degree in mathematics, linguistics, or computer science. Cryptology courses may be offered within any of these majors. Classes in foreign languages, political science, international relations, and telecommunications are also helpful. However, mathematics is the most important subject to study. Many positions, especially those in academia, also require a master's degree or PhD in cryptology or mathematics.

Certification and Security Clearance

In civilian roles, certifications help cryptologists prove their skill level. For example, the EC-Council Certified Encryption Specialist covers cryptography skills. However, general information security certifications are more helpful and more widely recognized. Certified Information Systems Security Professional and CompTIA Security+ are two of the best ones to consider. Cryptologists who work for the military, government, or a national intelligence organization will likely need to obtain government security clearance. In the United States three levels of security clearance exist: confidential, secret, and top secret. Each level gives access to more sensitive information. The process to get clearance includes background checks and personal interviews with family, friends, and coworkers that attempt to determine the person's loyalty to the country and willingness to protect classified information.

Internships

An internship is an excellent way to begin a career in cryptology. In the United States the NSA and CIA both offer internships in intelligence, mathematics, information assurance, and more. Major companies including Microsoft also offer internships in cryptology or cryptography.

Skills and Personality

Most cryptologists love solving puzzles. "I really enjoy that process of looking at obfuscated data and being able to pluck out shades of meaning. It's the same thing that happens when you're solving a puzzle," says Roger B. The types of puzzles that face these professionals are particularly complex and challenging. Successful cryptologists are highly intelligent, are inquisitive, and pay close attention to detail.

The job requires very strong math and statistical analysis skills, such as number theory, algebra, information theory, and probability. An understanding of computer science is also important. People who speak or enjoy learning foreign languages should also consider this profession. Cryptologic technician positions in the US Navy require fluency in at least one of the following languages: Spanish, Russian, Korean, Chinese, Arabic, or Persian.

On the Job

Employers

The companies that hire cryptologists are the ones that need to protect sensitive data. These include technology and communications companies, such as Google and Microsoft, and also financial services companies, such as PayPal or major credit card companies. Government intelligence agencies such as the FBI, CIA, and NSA in the United States also hire cryptologists, as do law enforcement agencies, the US Navy, and other military branches. Cryptologists in academic research positions often work at colleges, universities, or research centers.

Working Conditions

Most cryptologists work indoors in an office or laboratory with computers and other high-tech equipment. The job requires the ability to focus for long hours on a particular problem. Though cryptologists may work together as a team, they often spend a great deal of time working through complex problems by themselves. However, the job offers the satisfaction of knowing that the work matters. In the NSA Careers video, a cryptanalyst using only her first name, Laura, says, "It's nice to do something meaningful, to go into work and know you have a purpose. It's to protect Americans from outside forces that would do them harm." Cryptologists who work for the US government may need to relocate to Washington, DC.

In the navy, cryptologic technicians usually live on ships and travel constantly. Barbee says, "I've been able to travel all over the world. I've been to the Middle East. I've been to France, Italy, and Spain." Other military roles in cryptology also require deployment to foreign countries.

Earnings

Cryptology is a specialty area within mathematics. According to the Bureau of Labor Statistics, the median annual wage for mathematicians is $103,010. Cryptologists tend to make less than this, especially in entry-level positions. In an entry-level position for the government, a cryptologist would likely make between $35,000 and $50,000 per year. At a private company, compensation tends to be higher, from about $45,000 to $60,000 yearly, according to BankInfoSecurity. A master's degree, PhD, or several years of work experience can easily boost a cryptologist's salary to over six figures.

Opportunities for Advancement

It may be difficult to find an entry-level cryptology position. Starting out as a software engineer or computer systems analyst is a great first step into the private sector. After working for five or more years and obtaining an advanced degree, many more options open up in this field. Midcareer positions include cryptography researcher or cryptography engineer. A focus on management may lead to senior-level positions such as chief security officer.

In academia, cryptologists start out as PhD students and then become visiting, assistant, or associate professors. The ultimate goal is to get tenure, or a permanent job within an academic institution.

In the military, rank is well defined. In the navy, for example, successful cryptologic technicians will move through the naval ranks from seaman recruit up through petty officer, chief petty officer, and perhaps all the way up to lieutenant, captain, or admiral. Barbee worked his way up through the navy because he sought out opportunities for training and education. "I started in the engine room working with engines and tools, and now I'm working on intelligence reports that could make it to the president," he says.

What Is the Future Outlook for Cryptologists?

For most of the twentieth century, cryptologists could only find work in the military or with a government intelligence agency. The job focused only on encoding and decoding secret government and military transmissions. The rise of digital technology has changed this field dramatically. Almost every transfer of information between digital devices and the Internet uses some form of encryption and decryption. As the Internet of Things grows, objects that communicate with each other and with the cloud will increasingly utilize encryption and decryption to protect user data. Cryptocurrency is another emerging technology that depends on cryptology.

Cryptologists are in high demand to assist with all of these technologies. "Data encryption and security is a huge and growing field today," says cryptologist Rainer Steinwandt in an article on the BankInfoSecurity website. "New companies pop up daily that need to have data encrypted; they do that with software and 'keys' developed by cryptologists using mathematics." Those individuals interested in a career as a cryptologist should find ample job opportunities in this ever-expanding field.

Armed Forces Communications and Electronics Association (AFCEA)
4400 Fair Lakes Ct.
Fairfax, VA 22033
website: www.afcea.org

The AFCEA is a nonprofit professional organization that encourages collaboration among military, government, and industry communities in order to advance information technology, communications, and electronics capabilities.

Crypto Currency Certification Consortium
website: https://cryptoconsortium.org

This organization offers training and certifications for professionals who wish to gain expertise in cryptocurrency technology, including Bitcoin and Blockchain.

International Association for Cryptologic Research
website: www.iacr.org

This nonprofit organization supports and promotes the science of cryptology. The group organizes conferences, symposia, and training schools to help advance the field of cryptology.

National Cryptologic Museum
8290 Colony Seven Rd.
Annapolis Junction, MD 20701
website: www.nsa.gov/about/cryptologic-heritage/museum

This museum located next to the headquarters of the NSA shares the legacy of cryptology in US history. Visitors learn about people who devoted their lives to cryptology and national defense.

Interview with an Information Security Architect

David Hayes began his career as a lieutenant in the US Army. For three years in the 1980s, he worked at the Pentagon as a computer systems manager. For the past twenty-five years, he has worked on information security at Verizon and currently holds the title principal member of technical staff. He spoke with the author about his career.

Q: Why did you become an information security architect?
A: I sort of happened into it by accident. I was about ten years old, and I was doodling computer pictures all over my homework papers. A very astute math teacher, Mr. Charles Lamb, found the pictures and got me to the local college to see their computer—a machine that at the time cost as much as every house on my block. A kindly college administrator, Robert Taylor, allowed me my first experiences using the college computer system. There was never any part of the computer I could not explore. If it had not been for their encouragement and some gentle steering, my life today would be very different.

Q: Can you describe your typical workday?
A: My daily work covers two areas, in about equal proportions. I lead a team of five who build and operate the machines that watch for attackers inside Verizon. About 450 of these machines, called Intrusion Detection Systems, look for patterns that represent unusual or improper activity and create over 2 million alerts each day. The attackers, whom we call "black hats" after the

bad guys in cowboy movies, constantly develop new attacks. We must continually update our systems to keep pace. That's difficult when you work for a telecommunications company. The telephone network is never allowed to stop, the Internet is always busy, and 911 phone calls must go through every single time.

The other half of each day is taken up with creating the security standards that guide other engineers in Verizon. It's not possible to be perfectly secure, so I have to figure just how close we should try to come. Good security rules are a careful balance between how much risk we face from the black hats, and how much effort and expense is required to protect against it. I spend a lot of time researching new developments and understanding the most technical depths of how things like e-commerce web pages really work. Learning new things is fun, and I get to see my learning applied to help protect one of the largest networks in the world.

Q: What do you like most about your job?
A: The people I get to work with. Because it's Verizon, we can afford to get some of the very best in the world at this task. I respect their abilities and they respect mine. Feeling respected and valued in your work is incredibly important.

Q: What do you like least about your job?
A: Occasionally I will run into a fight with somebody who says, "I don't want to follow this rule because it's inconvenient." Guess what, having to unlock your car is inconvenient, especially if you've forgotten your keys. But it's a whole lot better than getting your car stolen! People who have the view that I don't want to do this because it makes my work more difficult—I have a tough time dealing with that. It doesn't happen very often but is annoying when it does.

Q: What personal qualities and skills do you find most valuable for this type of work?
A: Logic, and there's an element of integrity that is important. Bad things will happen, and if you make a mistake, you have to be willing to own it. In terms of what you need to know, the most useful skill that I have used every day in my work has nothing to do with

computers. It's English, basic written communication. No matter how brilliant you are, if you can't share your ideas with anyone else, they die with you.

Q: What is the best way to prepare for this type of job?
A: These days there are formal courses of study you can go through [to get into information security]. That was not the case when I did it. The concept of computer security did not exist. The Internet hadn't been invented. These days, at the college level, you'd want to take a course in information security. And there are certifications from vendors that say you are an expert with their product. Microsoft and Cisco are two of the best known. That's great if you're going to be operating a security system. And that's probably where you'll start, as an operator. You need to understand how the systems are used before you can understand how they're abused.

Q: What other advice do you have for students who might be interested in this career?
A: Find a mentor. Talk to your teachers, tell them you have an interest, ask if they can help you find somebody who can show you more about the security world. I'd love to see kids get more into this. It is such a fun area to work in. Every day there's something going on that didn't happen before. If you like always having a new challenge, this is a wonderful place to work.

Other Jobs in Cybersecurity

Chief information security officer

Computer crime investigator

Computer forensic analyst

Computer network defense analyst

Cryptanalyst

Cryptography researcher

Cybersecurity police officer

Cyber threat analyst

Data privacy officer

Data privacy specialist

Electronic warfare specialist

FBI special agent, cyber division

Health information privacy specialist

Information assurance engineer

Information assurance specialist

Information security manager

Information security policy and risk analyst

Internet security specialist

Malware analyst

Network administrator

Network security architect

Penetration tester

Risk assessor

Security consultant

Security software developer

Security systems administrator

Software engineer

System administrator

Vulnerability researcher

Editor's note: The US Department of Labor's Bureau of Labor Statistics provides information about hundreds of occupations. The agency's *Occupational Outlook Handbook* describes what these jobs entail, the work environment, education and skill requirements, pay, future outlook, and more. The *Occupational Outlook Handbook* may be accessed online at www.bls.gov/ooh.

Index

Note: Boldface page numbers indicate illustrations.

Active Directory (Windows tool), 9
Adhikari, Avishek, 68
Alert Logic, 9
Alexander, Candy, 19
American Bar Association (ABA), 56
Anderson, Robert, Jr., 48
Armed Forces Communications and Electronics Association
   (AFCEA), 73
Association of Certified Fraud Examiners, 65
Atlantic (magazine), 30

BankInfoSecurity (website), 71, 72
Barbee, Steve, 68, 71, 72
Big Four accounting firms, 62–63, 64
"black hats," 4–5, 74–75
blue teams, 25, 34
Boardman, Ruth, 55
Bourke, Triona, 60
Bowens, O'Shea
   on blue team exercises, 34
   on career advancement as cyber incident responder, 39
   on personal skills needed by cyber incident responders,
     36–37
*Breaking into Information Security: Crafting a Custom Career
   Path to Get the Job You Really Want* (Meyers), 35
Bugcrowd, 29
Bureau of Labor Statistics (BLS)
   cybersecurity career possibilities, 77
   earnings of mathematicians, 71
   job outlook
     accountants and auditors, 64
     information security analysts, 14
     lawyers, 55

Capture the Flag events, 31
Career Corner, The (podcast), 51
Cassidy, Richard, 9
Centre for Information Policy Leadership, 56
certification and licensing
   cryptologists, 67, 69
   cyber incident responders, 33, 35–36
   data privacy attorneys, 50, 52
   digital forensics investigators, 42, 45
   ethical hackers, 25, 27
   information security analysts, 8, 11
   information security architects, 16, 18
   security auditors, 58, 60–61
Certified Ethical Hacker (CEH) certification, 27, 30, 32
Certified Fraud Examiner certification, 60, 65
Certified Information Privacy Professional certification, 52
Certified Information Security Manager (CISM) certification, 18
Certified Information Systems Auditor (CISA) certification, 60,
   62
Certified Information Systems Security Professional (CISSP)
   certification, 11, 36, 69
Certified in Risk and Information Systems Control (CRISC)
   certification, 11, 60
Certified Internal Auditor certification, 60

Certified Network Defender (CND) certification, 35, 40
Certified Secure Software Lifecycle Professional (CSSLP)
   certification, 18
Chapman University, 5
Compact (magazine), 64–65
CompTIA, 13, 14
CompTIA Security+ certification, 11, 69
Computer Hacking Forensic Investigator (CHFI) certification, 45
computer security incident response teams (CSIRTs), 38–39
cryptanalysis, described, 67
Crypto Currency Certification Consortium, 73
cryptography, described, 67
cryptologists
   advancement opportunities, 71–72
   basic facts about, 67
   career paths, 67–68
   certification and security clearance, 69
   earnings, 71
   educational requirements, 69
   employers, 68, 70
   information sources, 73
   internships, 70
   job description, 67–68, 71
   job outlook, 72–73
   personal skills and qualities, 70
CSO (website), 34, 38
CSO from IDG, 40
cyberattackers, 4–5
cybercrime, difficulty of protecting against, 5
cyber incident responders
   advancement opportunities, 39
   basic facts about, 33
   certification and licensing, 35–36
   earnings, 39
   educational requirements, 35
   employers, 37–38
   information sources, 40–41
   job description, 33–35, **37,** 38–39
   job outlook, 40
   mentors for, 36
   networking and internships, 36
   other terms for, 33
   personal skills and qualities, 36–37
CyberPatriot: The National Youth Cyber Education Program,
   31, 48–49
cybersecurity, importance of, 4
Cybersecurity Ventures, 7, 40

data encryption programs, 9
data privacy attorneys
   advancement opportunities, 55
   basic facts about, 50
   certification and licensing, 52
   earnings, 54–55
   educational requirements, 52
   employers, 53–54
   information sources, 56–57
   job description, 50–51, 54
   job outlook, 55–56
   networking and internships, 53

personal skills and qualities, 53
volunteer work, 53
DEF CON, 31
digital crime, described, 43
digital devices and technology, 4, 6
digital forensics investigators
    advancement opportunities, 47–48
    basic facts about, 42
    certification and licensing, 45
    earnings, 47
    educational requirements, 44
    employers, 46
    information sources, 48–49
    job description, 42–44, **46,** 47
    job outlook, 48
    mentors for, 45
    networking and internships, 45
    personal skills and qualities, 45–46
DiMino, André, 43–44
Dumas, David
    on earnings, 13
    on need for information security analysts, 14
    on need for information security architects, 23
    on networking, 11

earnings
    cryptologists, 67, 71
    cyber incident responders, 33, 39
    data privacy attorneys, 50, 54–55
    digital forensics investigators, 42, 47
    ethical hackers, 25, 29–30
    information security analysts, 8, 13
    information security architects, 16, 21
    security auditors, 58, 63
    top cities for cybersecurity salaries, **6**
EC-Council, 31–32, 40, 49
EC-Council Certified Encryption Specialist certification, 69
educational requirements
    cryptologists, 67, 69
    cyber incident responders, 33, 35
    data privacy attorneys, 50, 52
    digital forensics investigators, 42, 44
    ethical hackers, 25, 27
    information security analysts, 8, 10–11
    information security architects, 16, 17–18
    security auditors, 58, 60
Elazari, Keren, 31
employers
    cryptologists, 68, 70
    cyber incident responders, 37–38
    data privacy attorneys, 53–54
    digital forensics investigators, 46
    ethical hackers, 29
    information security analysts, 12
    information security architects, 20
    security auditors, 62–63
ethical hackers
    advancement opportunities, 30
    basic facts about, 25
    career path to becoming, 27
    certification and licensing, 27
    earnings, 29–30
    educational requirements, 27
    employers, 29
    information sources, 31–32
    job description, 17, 25–26, 29
    job outlook, 30–31
    networking and internships, 27–28
    personal skills and qualities, 28

Fijneman, Rob, 64–65

financial costs, 5
firewalls, 9
Flatley, Christopher M., 10, 11
Forum of Incident Response and Security Teams (FIRST), 41
Future of Privacy Forum, 56

General Data Protection Regulation (2018, EU), 51, 55–56
GIAC Certified Forensic Analyst (GCFA) certification, 45
GIAC Certified Forensic Examiner (GCFE) certification, 45
GIAC Certified Incident Handler (GCIH) certification, 35
GIAC Penetration Tester (GPEN) certification, 27
GIAC Security Essentials (GSEC) certification, 11
GIAC Security Leadership (GSLC), 18
GIAC Systems and Network Auditor certification, 60
Global CyberLympics, 28
Global Information Security Workforce Study, 22–23
Grafenstine, Theresa, 64
    on earnings, 63
    job description of security auditors, 58
    on volunteering, 61
Grant, Hazel, 54

HackerOne, 29
hacking competitions, 28, 31
Halai, Sailesh, 59, 60, 63
Hayes, David, 18–19, 74–76
Health Insurance Portability and Accountability Act (1996),
    50–51, 59
Help Net Security (website), 26
Henley, Debbie, 38, 40
Herjavec, Robert, 6–7
Hurley, Deborah, 21

information security analysts
    advancement opportunities, 13–14
    basic facts about, 8
    certification and licensing, 11
    earnings, 13
    educational requirements, 10–11
    employers, 12
    information sources, 14–15
    job description, 8–10, 12–13
    job outlook, 14
    networking and internships, 11
    other terms for, 8
    personal skills and qualities, 12
information security architects
    basic facts about, 16
    career path to becoming, 22, 76
    certification and licensing, 18
    earnings, 21
    educational requirements, 17–18
    employers, 20
    information sources, 23–24
    internships and volunteer work, 18–19, 76
    job description, 16–17, **19,** 21, 74–75
    job outlook, 22–23
    mentors for, 19, 76
    personal skills and qualities, 19–20, 75–76
    work experience requirements, 16
Information Systems Security Association (ISSA), 15, 23
Institute of Internal Auditors (IIA), 65
International Association for Cryptologic Research, 73
International Association of Computer Investigative Specialists,
    49
International Association of Privacy Professionals, 57
International Information System Security Certification
    Consortium [(ISC)²], 15, 23, 36, 41
International Organization for Standardization (ISO), 65–66
International Society of Forensic Computer Examiners, 49
Internet of Things (IoT), 56

internships. *See* networking and internships
Intrusion Detection Systems, 74
Irvine, John
    on high turnover rate in digital forensics investigation, 47
    on internships and mentors, 45
    on job description of digital forensics investigators, 43
    on personal skills of digital forensics investigators, 45–46
ISACA, 23–24, 60, 66
ISO/IEC 27001 certification, 59
ISO/IEC 27001 Lead Auditor certification, 61
IT Governance (website), 59

job descriptions
    cryptologists, 67–68, 71
    cyber incident responders, 33–35, **37,** 38–39
    data privacy attorneys, 50–51, 54
    digital forensics investigators, 42–44, **46,** 47
    ethical hackers, 17, 25–26, 29
    information security analysts, 8–10, 12–13
    information security architects, 16–17, **19,** 21, 74–75
    security auditors, 58–59, 63
job outlook, 7
    cryptologists, 67, 72–73
    cyber incident responders, 33, 40
    data privacy attorneys, 50, 55–56
    digital forensics investigators, 42, 48
    ethical hackers, 25, 30–31
    information security analysts, 8, 14
    information security architects, 16, 22–23
    security auditors, 58, 64–65
Johnson, Mark, 43

Kimmel, Chris, 42

Lamb, Charles, 74
Lawyer (website), 54, 55
licensing. *See* certification and licensing
Lifehacker (blog), 26, 38–39

Magarasevic, Jelena, 18, 20
mentors
    for cyber incident responders, 36
    for digital forensics investigators, 45
    for information security architects, 19, 76
Meyers, John, 35
Miller, Ben, 26, 38–39
minorities, in cybersecurity workforce, 13, 21
MIS Training Institute, 66
Mitchell, Tenisha, 36

National Association for Law Placement, 57
National Cryptologic Museum, 73
networking and internships
    cryptologists, 70
    cyber incident responders, 36
    data privacy attorneys, 53
    digital forensics investigators, 45
    ethical hackers, 27–28
    information security analysts, 11
    information security architects, 18–19, 76
    security auditors, 61
Norris, Kate, 51

Occupational Outlook Handbook (Bureau of Labor Statistics), 77
Offensive Security, 32
Offensive Security Certified Professional (OSCP) certification, 27
Ostrowski, Steven, 13

PayScale

about, 21
earnings of
    cyber incident responders, 39
    data privacy attorneys, 54–55
    information security architects, 21
    security auditors, 63
penetration testing, 25
personal skills and qualities
    cryptologists, 67, 70
    cyber incident responders, 33, 36–37
    data privacy attorneys, 50, 53
    digital forensics investigators, 42, 45–46
    ethical hackers, 25, 28
    information security analysts, 8, 12
    information security architects, 16, 19–20, 75–76
    security auditors, 58, 62
picoCTF, 32
PricewaterhouseCoopers, 5
privacy law specialists, 52

Rabinowitz, Peter A., 53
Redlinger, Tony, 62
red team testers, 20, 29
    See also ethical hackers
Rivera, Fatima, 17
r00tz Asylum, 28, 31

Sanchez, Tony, 8, 14
SANS Institute
    information about, 15, 24, 41
    size of companies with cyber incident responders, 38
Schlemmer, Jason, 12
security auditors
    advancement opportunities, 64
    basic facts about, 58
    certification and licensing, 60–61
    earnings, 63
    educational requirements, 60
    employers, 62–63
    information sources, 65–66
    job description, 58–59, **61,** 63
    job outlook, 64–65
    personal skills and qualities, 62
    volunteering and internships, 61
security operations centers (SOCs), 38
Sherman, Rob, 34, 36, 38
Sokanu (career-matching platform), 60
Solove, Daniel, 53
Steinwandt, Rainer, 72

Taylor, Roger, 74
Times of India (website), 68
Trigo, Clifford, 30

U.S. News & World Report (magazine), 14

Vincent, Peter, 22
volunteer work. *See* networking and internships

Watson, Aaron, 47
Westman, Shelley, 22, 55
Wheeler, Tom, 4
white hat hackers. *See* ethical hackers
women, in cybersecurity workforce, 13, 21
Women's Society of Cyberjutsu, 15

Yahoo!, 4
Yeo, John, 26

Zinghini, Frank, 7